SIMPLE THINGS YOU CAN DO TO IMPROVE YOUR PERSONAL FINANCES

ALSO BY ILYCE R. GLINK

100 Questions You Should Ask About Your Personal Finances

100 Questions Every First-Time Home Buyer Should Ask

100 Questions Every Home Seller Should Ask

10 Steps to Home Ownership

50

SIMPLE THINGS YOU CAN DO TO IMPROVE YOUR PERSONAL FINANCES

How to Spend Less, Save More, and Make the Most of What You Have

Ilyce R. Glink

THREE RIVERS PRESS

NEW YORK

This book is intended as a general guide to the topics discussed, and it does not deliver accounting, personal finance, or legal advice. It is not intended, and should not be used, as a substitute for professional advice (legal or otherwise). You should consult a competent attorney and/or other professionals with specific issues, problems, or questions you may have.

Company names, logos, and trademarks used in the book belong to the companies that own them. There is no attempt to appropriate these names, logos, and trademarks, and none should be construed. Also, there is no endorsement, implied or otherwise, of the companies listed in this book. They are used to illustrate the types of places, software, or information centers where readers can find more information. Finally, company names, phone numbers, addresses, and Web sites may have changed since the publication of this book.

If you wish to contact Ilyce Glink, visit her Web site, www.thinkglink.com.

Published by Three Rivers Press, New York, New York.
Member of the Crown Publishing Group.

Random House, Inc. New York, Toronto, London, Sydney, Auckland
www.randomhouse.com

THREE RIVERS PRESS is a registered trademark and the Three Rivers Press colophon is a trademark of Random House, Inc.

Printed in the United States of America

Design by Publications Development Company of Texas

Library of Congress Cataloging-in-Publication Data

Glink, Ilyce R., 1964–
    50 simple things you can do to improve your personal finances : how to
spend less, save more, and make the most of what you have / Ilyce R. Glink.
        p. cm.
    Includes index.
    1. Finance, Personal.   I. Title: Fifty simple things you can do to
improve your personal finances.   II. Title.
HG179.G5519   2001
332.024—dc21   00-066675

ISBN 0-8129-2742-7

10 9 8 7 6 5 4

First Edition

For Sam, Alex, and Michael
Who remind me every day that the
simple things in life are best.

Contents

CHAPTER 3   Credit, Credit Reports, and Debt

CHAPTER 4   Investing Yourself in Your Investments

CHAPTER 5   Big Purchases: Cars, Homes, College Tuition, and Weddings

Preface

Throughout the ages, money (or any of its substitutes like gold, silver, precious gems, spices, barter services, tea, etc.) has played a central role in our lives. We've gone to great lengths to earn it, steal it, hoard it, protect it (was Fort Knox really necessary?), save it, invest it, spend it frivolously, use it wisely, and give it away.

We've always had trouble with it. And have we ever really known how to talk about it?

50 Simple Things You Can Do to Improve Your Personal Finances will help you spend less, save more, and make the most of what you have. The Simple Things I suggest you do in this book are designed to help you develop the financial common sense that comes naturally to people of great wealth. The tips labeled "A Good Start" will give you a starting point. While some of these suggestions may seem intuitive, others may be more difficult for you to adopt.

Don't despair. Over time, all of these Simple Things and more will come to you as naturally as if you'd been taught them in grade school—which is where the basics of personal finance *should* be taught.

Remember, money won't buy you happiness. It just gives you options. The rest is up to you.

Ilyce R. Glink

P.S. If you'd like to share some of your money tips, horror stories, and savings suggestions, or if you just have a question, contact me through my Web site, www.thinkglink.com.

Introduction

The best things in life are free. Money will buy the rest—if you can get your hands on enough of it.

But the truth is, most of us aren't looking to be as wealthy as some of the new dot-com billionaires. I wouldn't know what to do with that kind of cash (although I admit it would be nice to have the chance to try to figure it out). All we want is to have enough cash to pay the bills, fund our retirement, and to play a little.

The good news is that having enough money to achieve your financial goals is within your reach. The 50 Simple Things in this book will help you take control over what comes in and where you spend it. You'll feel better because you're taking an active role in managing your money and the issues it brings to your daily life. And you'll have the deep satisfaction of seeing your world change as you want it to.

Start today. Today is the best day ever to start improving your personal finances. Tackle these Simple Things one at a time. Integrate each of the "A Good Start" tips into your life before you tackle the next one. Think of them together as a ladder, each of the tips being another rung that will lead you toward financial freedom.

No one manages his or her money perfectly; everyone blows a few bucks now and then on junk. The trick is to manage your money well enough so that it gets you where you want to go.

Let's get going.

SIMPLE THINGS YOU CAN DO TO IMPROVE YOUR PERSONAL FINANCES

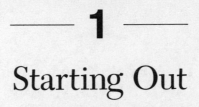

Starting Out

SIMPLE THING

1

CREATE A PERSONAL FINANCE SPACE (AND STREAMLINE YOUR FINANCIAL LIFE)

Unless you're naturally organized (and I'll admit up front that I don't qualify), the first thing to do that will drastically improve your personal finances is to get organized. And the best way to do this is to create a personal finance space.

Ideally, your personal finance space will have a place for unpaid bills and receipts, your household files, pens, stamps and envelopes, and other items you'll need to keep track of your money and investments.

Clearly a shoe box won't work. Instead, head over to your local office-supply store (like Staples, Office Max, or Office Depot), or Wal-Mart or Target. At stores like these, you'll find desk-high, plastic filing cabinets and six-drawer organizers on wheels. At press time, these cost less than forty dollars.

If you can afford it, purchase one filing cabinet with two drawers, and one six-drawer organizer. If you can only afford to purchase one, purchase a configuration that gives you two drawers for your supplies (the envelopes, stamps, pens, and paper) and one filing cabinet.

You may also want to purchase a package of letter-size manila folders (they cost less than five dollars for a package of one hundred), and a package of folder hangers (also less than five dollars per package of twenty-five, and they come in nice colors).

Making the Most of Your Personal Finance Space

Now that you've got your organizers, find or buy your pens, paper, stapler, staple remover, calendar, calculator, stamps, envelopes, paper, and paper clips. These and other supplies go into the six-drawer organizer, or in the top two drawers of the single organizer.

In the bottom, you'll want to create a series of files that will ultimately hold all your paid and unpaid bills, account statements, stock purchase or sale confirmations, warranties, and any other records that seem important to keep.

The total cost for organizing your finances will be either less than a hundred dollars (if you purchase two plastic filing cabinets) or less than fifty dollars (if you purchase one). But the best part is this: Once you've created a space for organizing your personal finances, you'll find it a lot easier to wander over and pay your bills, check on your stock portfolio, and take care of your money.

A GOOD START

The whole idea behind organizing your personal finances is to streamline your financial life. This means not only keeping all of the paperwork in one place, but slowly re-organizing your finances so that instead of having ten mutual funds with ten different fund companies, you have three or four funds with the same company. Instead of having a bank account here and another one there, and another one in a different state, you'll have just the basic accounts you need in one place and be able to access them, eventually, online. The end result is that you'll have cut down your mail from ten monthly envelopes to one. (Saves you time and saves trees, too.)

If you have bank accounts and savings accounts and mutual fund accounts spread out all over the place, you need to begin the consolidation process by looking at everything all at once. Spread out your most recent statements and look at what you have and where it is.

Next, try to find a bank that offers you a good deal and excellent service, that is convenient to you, and has plenty of ATM machines (so you don't get charged for going outside the network). It might be near your office or near your home. Move all of your accounts (you need a checking account and a money market account) to this bank, so they're close to you and all in one place.

Moving right along, you should now find a high-quality mutual fund company or brokerage firm that you can work with to manage your investments. The nice thing about choosing a company like Vanguard, Fidelity Investments, or Charles Schwab is that they are online 24/7/365, and easily accessible with a toll-free phone call from just about anywhere. This isn't an endorsement of these companies, but I'm suggesting you'll want to keep these things in mind, as well as the fact that huge companies like these will be there when you get to retirement age, when it comes to selecting an investment house.

You will want to move your retirement accounts, CDs, stocks, and other investments to this one investment company. Within the company, there should be dozens, if not hundreds, of mutual funds and other investments from which you can choose. But at the end of the month, all of your investments should come in just one envelope, easily organized, and kept so that you'll be able to look up in an instant what you own and where it is.

THROW AWAY WHAT
YOU DON'T NEED

As a general rule, human beings are collectors. We collect everything from art, coins, crystal, and silver to faded Levi's, Beanie Babies, baseball cards, and Michael Jordan's old basketball shoes. We also save stuff we won't ever need and that has no intrinsic value whatsoever, like tickets from the first date with one's spouse.

But getting your finances in order means parting with some of these "treasures." You want to clear out the clutter, or at least simplify the paperwork that you're going to keep in your newly organized personal finance space.

Here's a list of important papers you should keep, why you need them, and when you can throw them away:

1. Federal and state income tax returns. Under current tax law, the Internal Revenue Service (IRS) may audit you for three to six years after you've filed your federal income tax return. While they can only ask for receipts for up to six years, depending on the situation, if they believe you intentionally failed to report income, or filed a fraudulent tax return, there is no statute of limitations. Your best bet is to keep a copy of your tax return each year, along with all of the backup information.

2. Investment information. You need to know three things about your investments: how much you paid for them, how much you sold them for, and what kind of annual returns you earned while you held them. When you buy or sell an investment, your brokerage company will typically send you a confirmation. Hold on to it. You'll ultimately need that information, plus the dividend statements for your stock and mutual fund investments.

3. Retirement account records and paycheck stubs. If you've been making periodic contributions to an IRA, or if you've started a Roth IRA (see Simple Thing 47), there are certain tax records you should keep until you've withdrawn all funds from these accounts, to prove the amount of the nontaxable portion. Current tax law requires you to keep Forms 1040, 8606, 1099R, and 5498 for each year in which you made a contribution to your IRA accounts. Keep your paycheck stubs for each calendar year until you've received your W-2 form (usually in January) and checked it against your paycheck stubs for errors.

4. Insurance policies. You'll buy many different types of insurance in your life, including homeowner's, life, medical, auto, disability, and liability. You may even purchase various insurance policies for estate tax purposes. Keep the original insurance policy and signed contract for as long as you hold the policy. Once you cancel the insurance, you can throw out the policy papers about two years later.

5. Trusts and other estate-planning devices. Many individuals use trusts and other types of estate-planning tools to save on estate taxes. You'll need to keep trust documents, as well as backup documentation, for as long as those accounts are active.

6. Medical records. Current tax law permits you to deduct medical expenses in excess of 7.5 percent of your adjusted gross income (AGI). For example, if your AGI is $50,000, you may deduct the amount of medical expenses you paid that year in excess of $3,750, excluding medical insurance premiums. You'll want to keep all of your medical bills until the claim has been settled. If you have an ongoing medical situation, you may wish to keep these papers indefinitely, or until you've settled the claim. If you don't have enough medical bills to deduct anything from your tax return, toss them after you file your return—and be glad you're in relatively good health.

7. Credit card receipts and statements. Once you receive your monthly statement listing your most recent payment and any items purchased (or returned) since the previous statement, you can toss out the credit card receipts for that month's activity. (Of course, if you have your own business, different rules apply). But if you think you'll ever need a receipt, or if something has a "lifetime" warranty, you may want to hold on to it. If you're fighting with a store about an erroneous charge, or waiting for a store credit, you should keep your statements until that situation is resolved. Also, keep your receipt if you think you may want to return the item. After you've closed out your year and done your taxes, you can toss out your receipts at that point. If you're using financial software and don't need a receipt for tax purposes, to return an item, or for the warranty, you can toss the receipt as soon as you've entered it.

8. Household bills and receipts. It would be great if you could deduct the cost of food, heat, electricity, and diapers. Unfortunately, you can't. But you may be able to deduct the cost of child care or school tuition. After you've recorded the general household bills into your electronic software program or other expense ledger, you can toss them. Keep child-care receipts and tuition bills with your tax return files. If you qualify for a tax deduction, make those receipts part of your permanent tax records.

9. Canceled checks, ATM receipts, bank statements. Keep copies of your account statements, for IRS purposes, at least six years, and possibly forever. ATM receipts should be kept until the transactions they document show up on your bank statement. You can toss canceled checks after a year unless they document deductions or capital improvements.

10. Mortgage, home-equity loan, second mortgage, and property-tax records. Current tax law allows you to deduct interest paid on a first mortgage, a home-equity loan, or a second mortgage up to $1.1 million spread over two homes. You may also deduct your property taxes. Mortgage servicing companies will typically send you a year-end statement listing the amount of interest you've paid over the year, and the real estate and insurance premiums paid by the company on your behalf, if they escrow your tax and insurance payments. You'll need this statement and your property-tax bills when preparing your income tax return. After you file your return, it should become part of your permanent tax records.

11. Home purchase/sale and capital improvements records. Although current tax law permits you to take up to $250,000 in profits tax-free (up to $500,000 if you're married), you'll still want to hold on to your records so that you can prove exactly how you calculated your profits, and that may include records from prior home purchases and sales. These are documents you'll want to keep forever.

A GOOD START

Four of the most useful pieces of paper you should have on hand are

1. an updated list of your accounts and assets
2. a living will
3. a durable power of attorney for health care
4. a durable power of attorney for financial matters

Your "list of accounts" should include the name, account number, contact person (if available), phone number, and e-mail of every bank, mutual fund, stock, trust, and credit card account you own. List individual stocks and where the certificates can be found. List safe deposit accounts, life insurance policies (amounts and where they can be found), and any professionals who regularly assist you (such as brokers, attorneys, or accountants). Update this list annually and keep it in a safe place, like your safe deposit box.

A living will is a document that expresses what kind of medical treatment you want in case of a life-threatening illness or emergency in which you are unable to express your wishes directly. You can purchase a living will form at a stationery store, buy a book on writing one, use legal software to create one, or have an attorney write one for you. Make sure you and your spouse each sign living wills, and then tell your closest friends and relatives where your living wills can be found. Most important, give a properly completed copy of your living will to your doctor so he or she is aware of your wishes in case of a medical emergency.

A durable power of attorney gives someone you trust the power to make important decisions for you if you should become unable to do so. If, for example, you were in an accident and were in the process of selling your home, the person to whom you'd given a power of attorney would be able to complete the sale for you. Your attorney can guide you further.

INVEST IN A COMPUTER

When personal computers were first invented, back in the 1970s, it was tough to imagine that someday, there would be more computers in each home than people. We may not be there yet, but many of us have personal computers on our desks at work, on our tables at home, in our libraries and schools, and in our hands as we buzz about in our daily lives. (As of this writing, I confess to having five desktop PCs and a laptop in our home.)

But we're not all just playing games. We're e-mailing, shopping, browsing, learning, and, of course, playing. And those of us who are the most money-savvy are managing our money electronically.

If you don't already have a computer, you should spend the $500 it will cost to buy a fairly decent one (check the sale ads in your local paper on Sunday: I paid $400 for each of my most recent two computers). If you own a computer but aren't using it to track your finances, you're missing out. A computer can help you track your spending, balance your budget, mind your investments, and keep you abreast of the latest financial information.

In fact, there's more financial information online right now than you could ever use in a lifetime. Best of all, most of it is free!

So get online. Choose a money-management software program that suits you. If you choose Quicken (or

QuickBooks, if you have a small business), you can automatically download all of your information into Intuit's TurboTax program, which will help you do your own taxes quickly and easily.

But don't stop there. Get online and start tracking your investments electronically. You can sign on with a discount online broker, or go online with your regular brokerage company. You'll soon see that the time you spend maintaining your finances is minimal, but the rewards are well worth it. And using a computer is a whole lot more fun than trying to keep track of everything with a paper and pencil.

A GOOD START

The idea of using money management software can be daunting. There's lots of accounting gibberish and jargon built into these programs, which makes then feel inaccessible. Fortunately, Quicken and Microsoft Money have come a long way on usability. Best of all, there are plenty of books to give you a crash course on using these software programs to their best advantage.

Buy a copy of Quicken or Microsoft Money. Take an afternoon and input your account information, starting balances, stocks, and mutual funds. Pull out your receipts, and perhaps even your old checks (if you really want to start from the beginning of the year) and enter those, too. If you start off slowly—and I confess that at first Quicken had me totally befuddled!—and build steadily, you'll see that it's handy (if not downright fun) to know exactly where you are financially at all times.

SIMPLE THING

4

TAKE A DAY OF RECKONING

Many people find dealing with their finances daunting. They're not sure they're up to the task of managing of their money. So they pay a professional, or simply ignore the money realities of their life and hope for the best. While you can pay a professional to take care of some things for you—your taxes, for example—a true money manager or full-time financial planner may be beyond your means.

I firmly believe that *you* are the best person to manage your money. And I know you're capable of doing at least 95 percent of what needs to be done. But unless you streamline your financial life and make some smart choices early on, managing your money will be much more difficult and time-consuming.

Here's what you need to do. First, make sure your checking and money-market accounts are tied together so that you can transfer cash from the money-market account to your checking account by using the same ATM card. (Choose a bank with a large ATM network so you don't pay for each of these "transactions.")

Next, you'll want to choose a large financial services company that will be the central place you do business. You're looking for a company that offers brokerage accounts; a wide variety of well-respected mutual funds; and the ability to deposit cash electronically, use the Internet (reasonably cheaply) to trade online, search for information, and update your records. You want a company that's a known commodity and has a good reputation. Two good choices are Fidelity Investments and Charles Schwab, although there are others that meet this criteria.

The idea is to keep it simple. If you have multiple accounts at one financial institution, all of those accounts will be listed each month on a single statement. It will be far easier for you to keep track of your money because it will be in one place, not all over the map. By congregating your money in a single institution, you may also be able to take advantage of discounts available when your assets grow to reach certain levels.

For example, you might receive a discount on trading fees once you've accumulated a certain amount of assets at a financial institution, or you won't have to pay for funds kept in a retirement account. The institution might allow you to open a new account for a mutual fund with less than the minimum amount required, if you have significant assets invested elsewhere within the family of funds it operates. Keeping it simple will save you time and money.

A GOOD START

Do you find that you're a procrastinator by nature? Are you inclined to put off important jobs just because they don't seem easy?

Even if you have extremely complicated personal finances, you can get a running start if you give yourself a day (okay, half a day) of uninterrupted time. If possible, take a day off work when the kids are in school, or on the weekend when things are relatively quiet.

I'm going to assume you've done Simple Things 1, 2, and 3. You've organized your personal finance space, tossed old paperwork, purchased all your supplies, and bought a computer. If not, you can go online to staples.com, officemax.com, or officedepot.com and have the items you need for organizing your finances sent directly to your home.

When your day of reckoning comes, you want to be ready to dive right in. Put on some soothing music, pour a cup of coffee, and start separating the large stack of papers into smaller stacks of similar items. Put all bank, stock, and mutual-fund statements together. Put receipts into a different pile. Do the same thing with warranties, school reports, medical information, and other items.

Next, label your manila envelopes and put them alphabetically into your color-coded hanging files. Stick them into your plastic "home files" plastic tub. Then fill each individual file chronologically. You can organize from most recent to oldest statement or vice versa, as long as you're consistent. You may even want to create a hanging file for current catalogs from companies whose items you purchase on a fairly frequent basis, including gardening or office supplies.

Rubber-band old checkbook registers together and put them inside another hanging file. Keep old tax records together. While you're at it, take the holiday cards that have been sitting inside the basket since last December and sort through the ones you want to save and those you're ready to throw away. (Now, are you ready to tackle that box of snapshots?)

Remember, your day of reckoning is only a starting point. It's a way for you to build momentum and start moving in the right direction. And, it may take more than one day to sort yourself out.

But remember this: If you don't start organizing your finances, there's just going to be more to go through tomorrow.

CALCULATE YOUR
NET WORTH

Everyone should have a financial baseline. That is, you need to calculate your net worth—what you have minus what you owe—so that as your wealth grows through the years, you can easily track it (while remembering whence you came).

Figuring out how much you're worth is often eye-opening. Many times, people can't believe that they have a negative net worth—that is, they owe more than they own. And yet they continue to spend as if they have a million bucks in the bank. Knowing your bottom line can be a powerful motivator, particularly if you're struggling to keep your finances in line.

A quick formula for calculating how much you're actually worth is shown on page 18.

Now that you know how much you're worth, sit back and think about that number. Are you surprised by the bottom-line number? Do you feel that your net worth should be higher, given the amount of money you're earning?

Take a closer look at the numbers. What are your liabilities? What are your key assets? Are you spending too much? Saving too little? Every year, you should sit down and recalculate your net worth. If you buy a computer and

Your Net Worth

What You Own (Assets)	Approximate Cash Value Today
Cash	_____
Checking accounts	_____
Savings accounts	_____
Money market accounts	_____
Other accounts	_____
Treasury bills	_____
Cash value of life insurance	_____
Stocks and bonds	_____
Retirement accounts	_____
Real estate investments	_____
Personal assets (cars, furniture, jewelry, artwork, etc.)	_____
Total Assets	_____

What You Owe (Liabilities)	Amount
Mortgage	_____
Second home loan	_____
Home equity loan	_____
Credit card debt	_____
School loans	_____
Vehicle loans	_____
Miscellaneous debt (including personal loans, IRS debt, amount borrowed against retirement accounts, medical debts, etc.)	_____
Total Amount Owed	_____
Total Assets	_____
Total Liabilities –	_____
NET WORTH =	_____

track your finances online, you'll quickly be able to see where your net worth is at any given moment. But the idea is to watch that bottom number grow.

A GOOD START

Calculating your net worth is a big step. If you want to take the next stop, take a long, hard look at which assets make up your net worth.

Let's say your home equity accounts for 40 percent of your net worth (for some folks, it's as high as 60 to 70 percent), and you have about 10 percent in your checking account or money-market account, and the rest in retirement funds. This exercise tells you that the vast majority of your wealth is in your home, which doesn't do as much for you as wealth that is invested in the stock market. That's because real estate appreciates about 3 percent per year, on average. Over the last seventy years or so, the stock market has appreciated about 11 percent a year. But you don't want to put 100 percent of your money in the stock market (that would mean selling your home and renting), because that would be too risky.

Instead, you're looking for balance. About 30 to 40 percent of your wealth should be in your home (if you're twenty to twenty-five years or more away from retirement), while the rest should be invested in cash (your emergency fund, earning a nice rate in a money-market account or CD) or in the stock market.

Once you have input all the data, both Quicken and Microsoft Money will help you analyze your finances with a variety of cool pie charts and bar graphs, which makes it easy to see in "living color" exactly where you are financially.

DREAM BIG—AND WRITE DOWN
YOUR FINANCIAL GOALS

Make no small plans.

More than a century ago, architect and urban visionary Daniel Burnham suggested that the only way to make something happen was to dream big.

Of course, the same principle works with your personal finances. Nothing is going to happen until you visualize what you want to do with your wealth. Creating a written list of financial goals gives you a big brass (or is yours gold or perhaps platinum?) ring to grab for.

How do you create financial goals? They are nothing more than a wish list for your financial independence. Perhaps you want to be secure enough financially to quit your job and look for another. Or perhaps you want the flexibility to be a one-income family so that you or your spouse can stay at home and raise your kids.

Do you want to drive a nicer car? Buy a state-of-the-art stereo system? Take a vacation worth writing home about? Pay for your kids' college educations in cash? Retire at fifty-five?

All these things, and more, are possible. All you need is the vision to dream big, and the determination to get there.

A GOOD START

Dreaming is one thing. But writing down your financial goals brings them one important step closer to reality. Once you've committed yourself in writing, your dreams will feel that much more real—and achievable.

So pull out a sheet of paper and a pen (or if you've got your computer set up, open up a new file and label it "Financial Goals"), and begin writing down all your financial goals, no matter how small, petty, or short-term they may seem.

What are some sample goals? Perhaps you want your infant child to attend a prestigious private prep school. Or maybe you want to buy the latest Porsche. Do you want to add onto your house and create the home of your dreams? Or are you interested in taking a year off, as my cousin Sherri did for her fortieth birthday, and traveling the world?

Our goals are as individual as we are, and it's difficult to compare your financial goals with anyone else's. However, if you're married, or have a life partner, you must each create an individual list of goals.

Once your list (or lists) is created, it's time to prioritize. Separate your financial dreams into long-term and short-term goals. Set a time limit on when you want to achieve these goals. Set benchmarks on the way, so you will feel better achieving each milestone and know at any given time whether you're on track.

For example, if buying a home is at the top of your list, set a goal of having a certain amount of cash, like $3,000 or $5,000 for the down payment, in your house fund twelve months from the day you make the list. Set a benchmark three, six, and nine months down the line so you can see if your savings are growing as they should.

Simply by writing down and prioritizing your goals, you have increased substantially your odds of achieving them.

2

Budgets and Savings

LIVE BELOW YOUR MEANS

If you're looking for a magic formula that will make you rich beyond your wildest dreams, here it is: Spend less than you earn. It's the only way to start accumulating true wealth.

The problem is, we all struggle so much in our daily lives that we feel we richly deserve any convenience or nicety. And perhaps we do. But while spending on all the little things may feel good at that moment, it's hardly satisfying over the long run. Rarely will any book, video, or CD you buy today comfort you in your old age the way $1 million in cash will.

If you need motivation, go back to your list of financial goals. Remember, I encouraged you to dream big. For me, the most rewarding thing about living below my means is that my accumulated wealth gives me options. Based on what we already have saved, my husband, Sam, and I know we'll have the option of retiring early—if we want to take it. We'll have the means to travel, buy plants for our garden, take classes, go to dinner and the movies, lavish gifts on our children and (someday, we hope) grandchildren, and live the way we choose. And we'll still have some to pass down to the next generation.

Living below your means would seem easy to do. You just spend the same amount, even as your income rises. The problem is that as our income rises, there's always someplace that extra cash can go. There's always some new expense with kids, or maybe it's time to fix (or replace) your car. Homeowners know there's usually a house project that you've been putting off, or perhaps it's time to put down some cash on that vacation you've been planning. When you've paid all the other bills, there's usually some medical or dental expense waiting in the wings.

It's so hard to save above and beyond what we earn each month that we've become a nation that pays for our past expenses with future earnings—on our credit cards. The average person carries more than $4,000 in credit-card debt. A television reporter recently asked me this question: "Should I pay my taxes or my credit-card debt?" After she paid her taxes, she charged a $3,000 vacation on her credit card!

While it's easy to get financially lost in the aisles of some department store, it requires discipline to spend less and save more. But that's precisely what you have to do.

Start by tracking every cent you spend. If you followed my earlier suggestion to put your finances on a computer and use financial software like Quicken or Microsoft Money, your spending habits will be automatically tracked for you. All you have to do is generate a year-to-date report on your expenditures by clicking one button.

But if that seems too much right now, go out and buy a small notebook. Open it up and write the day and date at the top. Then start recording every cent you spend. Write down the cost of the newspaper you pick up on the way to the train, or the toll you pay when you drive to work. Write down how much you spend on the coffee and muffin you buy during your break, your lunch, your bus fare home, groceries, dry cleaning, dinner you order in, and the video you watch after you put the kids to sleep. Write down all of the bills you pay each month, from rent or mortgage to utility to medical to tuition.

At the end of each day, tally up the total at the bottom of the page. At the end of the week, tally up the total. At the end of the month, add up the last four weeks. Now compare it to your take-home pay. And ask yourself these two questions:

1. Am I spending more or less than I thought?
2. Am I spending more or less than I take home every month?

If you're like most folks, you'll be surprised at how much money you're spending each month. If you've got cash in your pocket, you'll probably find yourself spending it—mostly on the little things that bring instant gratification but are almost as instantly forgotten.

Again, the key to growing rich is to plug the hole in your pocket. And you'll do it by not spending on all the little things. Look at your spending record and see where your money goes. If you save just five dollars per week, you've saved $260 per year. Save one dollar per day and you'll have an extra $365 per year. Save $100 per month, and you'll end up with $1,200 per year. Invest that savings, and the wealth really starts to build.

A GOOD START

Here are ten quick things you can do that will immediately increase the balance in your checking account:

1. **Stop buying soda, candy, and cookies.** Tap water and fruit are far healthier choices, and often less expensive.
2. **Buy in bulk.** If you join a discount buying warehouse (like Sam's Club or Costco), you'll save not only money

but time. For example, you can spend $2.50 for a box of dishwashing soap at the grocery store, or $4.50 for a tub that will wash five times as many loads. The same goes for laundry detergent, olive oil, diapers, ketchup, crackers, etc. Do you buy fresh flowers to celebrate a special occasion? A dozen quality, long-stem roses will set you back anywhere from thirty to fifty dollars. At some wholesale clubs, you can get two dozen roses for half the price. But you need discipline. Do you really need the roses? You're not saving if you spend fifty dollars on a well-priced impulse purchase you don't need. And you have to know your prices, or you'll end up spending more on a bulk-size name-brand item than you would have on a generic item at a regular store.

3. **Purchase your auto and homeowner's insurance from the same company.** You may be entitled to a discount of up to 15 percent if you do. And while we're talking about insurance, raise your deductible. You may be able to shave another 15 to 30 percent off your annual costs.

4. **Adjust your thermostat.** By turning your thermostat up two degrees in summer and down two degrees in winter, you may be able to save more than 10 percent on your energy bills.

5. **Buy your food at the grocery store, not the coffee shop.** If you spend three dollars a day on a coffee and muffin/doughnut/croissant habit, you're spending fifteen dollars per week, or $780 per year. If you eat lunch out three times a week, that's an average of seven dollars per lunch, or twenty-one dollars per week, or nearly $1,100 per year. If you buy a

twenty-dollar coffee maker and buy expensive beans at ten dollars per pound, and drink it every day, you'll wind up saving plenty and you'll get your high-test designer coffee in the morning, too.

6. **Buy a used car.** Leasing a car is one of the worst ways to spend your money. It's expensive, the contracts are complicated, and at the end of your three years you wind up with nothing (or a bill for using up too many miles or ruining the condition of the car). Instead, buy a used car, preferably one that's still under factory warranty, and then keep it for seven to ten years.

7. **Rent a movie instead of going out to the movies.** I'm astonished at the cost of a movie ticket these days. For a family of four, plus one big bag of popcorn, you're looking at forty dollars or more (not including the cost of parking). If you leave the kids at home with a babysitter, and go out to dinner, that's a $100 evening. Save the big nights out for special occasions, and rent a movie (one dollar at my local library, free at many others) instead.

8. **Cook more.** It's so easy to buy pre-made food. Or order in a pizza. But you'll spend twice as much. Dinner for four at an inexpensive restaurant can easily exceed forty dollars. You could cook steak for a lot less! Make the time to cook your own food. If you cook on the weekends, prepare twice as much sauce, lasagna, stews, or soups as you need. Freeze the rest in serving-size containers. Then, during the week, pop it out of the freezer, and in thirty minutes you've got a home-cooked meal that is not only less expensive to prepare, but will probably taste better.

9. **Take public transportation.** If you have the option, you'll usually spend less on public transportation than you will if you drive to work and pay for parking. If there is no public transportation, consider carpooling at least once or twice a week.

10. **Change telephone companies.** Have you ever looked closely at your telephone bills? You're probably paying too much for your local or long-distance calls. It's often possible to cut your local and long-distance phone bill in half, simply by switching companies. The same is true for cellular phone service. Many folks consider a cell phone a necessity (I know I do). But that doesn't mean you have to pay through the nose for it. Start paying closer attention, and you'll probably find you can shave thirty to fifty dollars per month off your cell-phone bill.

There are plenty of other tips on saving money throughout this book, but if you just follow five of these ten suggestions, you'll wind up saving thousands of dollars per year—painlessly.

KICK A BAD HABIT

Let's face it—we're creatures of habit. Most of us like to do the same things, in the same way, each day. But as I mentioned earlier, one of the quickest ways to save a pile of change is to kick a bad habit.

Let's start at the top: Smoking a pack of cigarettes each day costs you at least four dollars, depending on where you live. That's twenty-eight dollars per week, or about $1,456 per year. And that price is only going in one direction.

A cup of gourmet coffee per day costs $3.50. Assuming weekdays only, that's $910 per year. Add in a bagel and cream cheese, and you can watch another $1.25 a day, or $325 per year, disappear from your wallet.

Here are the true costs of some other regular habits:

The True Cost of Daily Habits

Item	Cost Per	Cost per Year
Smoking (per pack)	$ 4/day	$1,456
Drink with the guys	10/week	520
Cable television	35/month	420
Coffee and muffin	2.75/day	715
Yard service	25/week	650 (6 months)
Lunch out	7/day	1,820

Item	Cost Per	Cost per Year
Weekly dinner and movie	50/day	2,600
Lottery tickets	5/week	260

Want to save money? Give up a daily, weekly, or monthly bad or unnecessary habit.

A GOOD START

A friend of mine recently lost fifteen pounds in two months. Her secret? "For the first time, I dieted and exercised at the same time," she said.

Sometimes you have to combine two or more things to achieve something meaningful. If you want to save a substantial amount of money, try eliminating two things from your daily budget, instead of just one.

Take the dollars and change you would have spent on such items as coffee and cigarettes out of your pocket and stick it in a jar. Every day, remove this amount of money and put it in the jar. After a month, you should notice two things: First, the jar is going to be pretty full. (Get ready for latte sticker shock.) Second, you probably aren't missing the items as much as you thought you might.

When you see that you're reaching your goals faster than the benchmarks you've set, the temporary sacrifices (permanent, hopefully, if you're kicking a cigarette habit) will be worth it.

SIMPLE THING

9

SAVE THE CHANGE

Psychologically, it helps to see how much you're saving each day. It feels really good to watch your money grow, especially if you have had to give up something tangible, like a cup of coffee or a restaurant dinner, in order to get there.

Here are two suggestions that should give you some immediate gratification while helping you save money:

First, every day I want you to empty your pockets or change purse of all change, plus one of the lowest denomination bills you're carrying that day. The next day, when you purchase something, break the lowest-denomination paper money you've got left.

The day I wrote this (it happened to be a Sunday), I emptied out my change purse and scraped up the additional change from the bottom of my purse. I found fifty-nine cents. I was carrying a one-dollar bill, a five-dollar bill, and a $100 bill (which I'd had in my wallet for about three weeks). Usually I have more change, but that's how it goes. Some days there's more, some days less. Some days your lowest bill is a dollar. Some days it'll be a five- or ten-dollar bill.

Following this suggestion, I'd put $1.59 into a jar. At the end of the month I'd have $47.70. At the end of the year I'd have $572.40. Want to beef it up? Take your two smallest bills and put them in the jar. Or, every time you pay for something, break a new bill. You'll end up with a chunk of change at the end of the day.

As an experiment, I did this recently. At the end of the month I had more than $100 in the jar. And I never missed the cash. The next day I'd simply break a new bill and start over again.

Here's the second suggestion: At the end of the month, take whatever cash you've accumulated and put it into your account. Write yourself a check for the amount and deposit it into your money-market account or, better yet, into a mutual fund or stock brokerage account.

A friend told me that she deposits her "savings" into a mutual fund account that makes it difficult, if not impossible, to withdraw any funds. Another woman I interviewed told me she puts her extra cash into a bank that's a half-hour drive from her house—and she didn't ask for an ATM card for the account.

If you save $100 per month this way, you'll have saved another $1,200 per year, plus interest on the cash you put away. Not only will you have painlessly put away this cash, but it will start to earn interest and grow on its own. And that's how you start to build real wealth.

A GOOD START

Create a graduated jar contribution schedule and stick to it. For the first month, take change only out of your wallet. For the second month, start removing your lowest-denomination bill plus the change. In the third month, remove two of your lowest-denomination bills (if it's two five-dollar bills, that's how it goes) plus the change. By the time you get to the fourth month, you should be able to remove the change, and the lowest- and second-lowest-denomination bill out of your wallet.

By then your jar will be bursting, and you'll have taught yourself this lesson: Most people only spend what's in their wallets. If you remove the cash, you remove the temptation to use it.

CREATE AN EMERGENCY FUND

Life happens. Your car breaks down. The roof leaks. Your kids get sick. Someone gets divorced. Someone loses a job. Someone dies.

When things happen, you need to be prepared. You have to be able to reach for the "mad money" your parents told you to take when you went out with your friends—if you got mad at them, you had enough cash to pay your own way home. It's the "rainy day" money, for when emergencies hit.

How much do you need? Most financial experts say you need to have enough cash in your emergency fund to cover two to six months' worth of expenses. So if your expenses are $2,000 per month, you'll need to have $4,000 to $12,000 stashed away just in case you have an emergency.

You should be able to tap into those funds relatively quickly, which means the best place for them is in a savings account. As you'll see in Simple Thing 12, I believe all of your money should work as hard as it can for you. So, instead of putting it into a regular passbook savings account that might pay only 2 percent on your money, you might want to put it in a money-market account, which might pay twice as much.

In any of these accounts, you can tap your cash at a moment's notice. If you have some money that's this liquid (which is investment jargon for completely accessible), you might want to salt away additional cash into a two-week certificate of deposit (CD), which may pay you more than a regular money-market account. While you'd only be able to tap this account every two weeks, that's a short enough period to make it workable for most emergencies.

A GOOD START

Once you've built up your reserve fund, you need to make the cash work as hard as it can for you. That means finding the best place to invest the money.

If you've saved up a three-month reserve of cash, and something unfortunate happens, it's unlikely you'll need all three months' worth of cash at once. It's entirely reasonable to put one month's worth into a two-month certificate of deposit (CD), which would then pay a higher interest rate than a simple money market account or savings account.

You can then work on saving up a fourth month of emergency reserve. For that, you might want to open up a brokerage account at one of the main investment companies, such as Fidelity Investments, Charles Schwab, or Vanguard. Each of those firms offers investors hundreds of mutual funds. What you might want to do is take the fourth month of reserve funds and put it into an index fund (Vanguard has the cheapest funds). Every month, instead of writing yourself a check and depositing it into your savings account, you'd send it off to your mutual-fund account.

The reason you do this with your fourth (and subsequent) month of savings is that mutual funds are a slightly riskier investment. Your funds are now at the whim of the market and will go up and down as the market rises and falls. However, over time, you will almost certainly earn a substantially higher rate of return on this investment, and you'll do so knowing that you still have three months of emergency reserve (the two months in your money-market account plus the one month in the CD) as a backup.

SIMPLE THING

11

PAY YOURSELF FIRST
AND LAST

How you pay your bills each month says a lot about how you feel about your personal finances. Do you pay each bill as it comes in, or do you let it linger until the bills pile up, and then attack the stack? Or do you stick the bills in a drawer and ignore them until your utility services are cut?

There's no single right way to pay bills. Some people pay them immediately. Some pay them every two weeks or once a month. The important thing is that you pay your bills on time. Paying late is the fastest way to lose money (late fees are expensive) and ruin your credit history.

One of the quickest ways to improve your finances, however, is to pay yourself first, before you pay a single bill. If you want to make it even more painless, consider having the funds withdrawn automatically from your account and deposited electronically into the account of your choice. No matter how frugal we think we are with our finances, if we have cash in our pockets (or in our checkbooks), we're more likely to spend it.

By writing out a check to yourself as soon as you receive a paycheck, and depositing it in a mutual fund or a money-market account, you're removing temptation. Most folks won't spend money they don't feel they have. So if you don't have it, your head is telling you not to spend. It helps put the brakes on impulse buying. (I usually do my impulse buying in the grocery store, where the damage is limited. A friend of mine used to go out for a walk on her lunch hour and come back with $100 worth of clothes three times a week. Now that kind of impulse buying can get expensive!)

If skimming $100 off the top of your check seems too easy, increase the amount. If you have money left over at the end of the month, write out another check to yourself for the difference and get it into your investment fund. If you leave the cash in your checking account and you know it's there, you're more likely to spend it on items you don't need.

So pay yourself first—and last. And while you're at it, pay your children second. Even if you put just twenty-five dollars per month away for their college educations, you'll find that cash growing a whole lot faster than if you left it in your checking account and frittered it away.

A GOOD START

Sometimes we forget to "pay ourselves" and the money goes to some other needy cause (like braces for our children, or new school clothes). It's easy to let these other legitimate expenses take priority—but don't let them.

Some people find it helpful to create invoices for themselves—"$250 to Fidelity" or "$100 to Schwab." In essence, you're creating a bill that literally sits in your bill pile and waits for you to pay it. Psychologically, having a physical piece of paper in front of you that says "Pay me now" might help get you over the hurdle and into the mode of saving cash each month.

MAKE YOUR MONEY WORK
HARDER FOR YOU

If you don't spend less than you earn, you'll never be rich. In fact, it will be difficult ever to achieve any financial stability whatsoever.

But to really start accumulating wealth, you need to make your money work as hard as it can for you. And that means putting it in places where it will earn the best return.

For example, most checking accounts don't pay interest. So the money you leave there to pay bills isn't earning anything. But almost all banks offer a money-market type of account that does earn interest. Keep most of your available cash in a money-market account at your bank, and when you're ready to pay your bills, transfer the money from the money-market account into your checking account.

Where should you keep your emergency reserve funds or additional cash you're saving? Put it in the account that pays the most interest.

For example, let's say your neighborhood bank offers a passbook savings account that pays 2 percent on funds. Two percent is better than stuffing your cash underneath your mattress. However, the average annual rate of inflation over the past thirty years has been around three percent. Basically, that means everything you buy will cost you 3 percent more next year than it does this year.

So if your cash is earning 2 percent and inflation is 3 percent, you're actually losing 1 percent of your money's buying power every year. You're losing money.

The next step up would be a money-market account. While these accounts often require a minimum of $1,000, they might pay 3 to 6 percent, depending on where interest rates are. At 3 percent, you're at break-even with inflation. Your cash (and buying power) will grow about as fast as the inflated cost of goods and services. If your money-market account is paying 4 percent, and inflation stays at 3 percent, you're actually earning a real return of 1 percent. (Actually, it's somewhat less than 1 percent because you'll probably pay tax on the earnings.)

That's better than nothing or losing money, but it isn't that great a return. You could put the cash into the stock market, say, in a stock mutual fund that's returned 20 percent per year for the past ten years. A 20-percent return is excellent. You could even go for a return of 10 percent (the stock market has returned, on average, a bit better than 11 percent per year for the past seventy years). That's why so many financial experts recommend putting your money into the stock market.

But the stock market is a long-term investment. You only want to invest funds there that you won't need for the next five to ten years. It isn't the place to put funds you'll need in the next two years, because stocks rise and fall (that's called volatility), and no one knows when that's going to happen.

But there is a place where you can get a little bit better return on your cash. Try putting your cash into a short-term CD or money-market account at a stock brokerage company. Such funds typically return 5 to 6 percent (when regular bank money-market accounts offer 3 percent) and the funds are liquid, meaning they're easily available to you if you need them.

What's the difference between getting a 3-percent return and a 6-percent return on your money? If you put away $100 per month, or $1,200 per year, the difference could be worth tens of thousands of dollars over the next thirty years.

A GOOD START

When you compare interest rates on your money at various financial institutions, look at the annual percentage rate (APR) as a point of comparison. The APR takes into account a standard amount of fees and interest, and calculates the total return on your investment. (And be sure to read the fine print for information about any penalties resulting from an early withdrawal of your cash.)

SIMPLE THING

13

MAKE TECHNOLOGY
WORK FOR YOU

Technology is moving so fast that soon you'll be able to manage all of your personal finances from a wireless, handheld computer permanently hooked up to the Internet. Or rather, you'll be managing your finances this way if you take advantage of existing, inexpensive technology and make it work for you.

Clearly, using a computer to handle your accounts and expenses is the first step. But you also need to get online to use the millions of pages of information available to you—mostly for free—through various Web sites operated by mortgage lenders, financial institutions, and companies that simply dispense financial news and advice.

Once you're there, you'll be able to access your accounts online and easily track your investments. You'll be able to buy and sell stocks or mutual funds inexpensively. You'll be able to manage your accounts quickly and easily. You'll be able to use online calculators to figure out how slowly or quickly you're meeting your investment goals.

And that's the real benefit of technology. It puts you more in control of your money by giving you access to the information and tools you need to manage your money effectively, from the mundane bill-keeping chores to planning for your future.

But once you've mastered the computer, money-management software, and the Internet, take the next step and incorporate a handheld organizer, like a Palm or Visor, into your life. Palms, which synchronize with your desktop system, can be enormously useful. You can put in your address list (and create labels for holiday cards and invitations). You can keep your daily calendar on hand with you. And you can keep track of to-do lists and daily expenditures. Soon you'll be able to connect to the Internet through your wireless handheld device, and comparison-shop through the Internet while you're at the bricks-and-mortar store looking at the item on the shelf.

A GOOD START

Use the Internet now to save money. Search for phone numbers (try Switchboard.com, or Yahoo! Yellow Pages) instead of paying for directory assistance (you'll save fifty-five to seventy-five cents per call). Use it to save time and obtain discounts online. There are sites that will give you grocery store coupons. Use it to compare prices between online e-tailers and local retailers. Services like mysimon.com or bottomdollar.com will link you to the cheapest e-tailer for a given product.

As you feel more comfortable, you can search for homes, loans, and travel tickets online. Once you start buying items from a Web site that also has a bricks-and-mortar presence, you may start receiving valuable coupons worth 25 to 50 percent off your next purchase. Just be sure you buy something you need, rather than go over budget just because you received a coupon online.

3

Credit, Credit Reports, and Debt

SIMPLE THING

14

IF YOU CAN'T PAY CASH, DON'T BUY IT

It's so easy to simply whip out a credit card to pay for everything from gas to groceries. And when you're pressed for time, it often seems that business is transacted more quickly when you hand over a credit card than when you pay in cash.

When you buy gas these days, most stations allow you to insert your credit card at the pump. If you pay cash, you need to go inside the station to settle the bill. That takes a few extra minutes. Ever tapped your foot impatiently while the customer at the front of the line paid for her groceries with a check instead of a credit card? Of course, you usually can't buy anything online unless you have a credit card.

It's certainly easier and faster to pay with a credit card these days. And that's where many folks get into trouble. It's too easy to forget how much you've already charged this month. It's too easy to just hand over the credit card and figure you'll worry about the bill later. It's too easy to pay the minimum each month and let the interest pile up.

It's much harder to live within your means. But paying cash (and that includes writing checks) will force you to do so. It will put the brakes on your spending habits.

When I was a child, I remember my grandfather paying in cash for just about every purchase. When the check came, he'd reach into his pocket and pull out a wad of crisp twenty-dollar bills. He'd peel off enough to pay the check, and then pocket the change.

Although my grandfather had a credit card (which he used only to rent cars when traveling), he believed that you should pay cash. If you couldn't afford to pay cash for something, he told me, you should wait until you could afford to do so.

It's simple but solid financial advice. And it stood my grandfather in good stead. An insurance salesman, he retired early, at age fifty-five. When he died twenty years later, he left an estate worth hundreds of thousands of dollars.

And you can, too.

A GOOD START

Start by figuring out how much cash you need to live each month. Continue to write checks for all of your regular bills, like rent and utility, and use your checkbook for big purchases such as groceries and clothes. For the rest of your weekly budget, take out the amount of cash you need and put it in a safe place. Then spend only that amount of money. (If you need a little extra help, stick your credit cards into a bag of water and freeze them.)

I'm often asked if folks should use a debit card rather than a credit card to make purchases. A debit card looks exactly like a credit card. The only difference is that it acts like a checkbook. You charge on a debit card and the amount is instantly withdrawn from your checking account.

The problem with debit cards is they offer few—if any—of the protections offered by credit card companies, with none of the credit benefits. So if your debit card gets stolen, you may have to cover all of the "charges" against your account. If your credit card gets stolen, you might only owe about $50.

If your debit card gets stolen and your account is emptied and checks you've already written against the account bounce, you'll probably owe extra fees to your bank to cover those bounced checks.

And, of course, you don't get to float your purchases for free (provided you're not carrying a balance on your credit card), you don't get miles or free cash or discounts against future automotive purchases, and you don't help your credit history.

So politely decline your bank's offer of a debit card. And if you can't use your credit cards responsibly, cut them up and close the accounts (in writing!).

SIMPLE THING

15

CONSOLIDATE YOUR LOANS

It's awfully tough to save anything when you're standing knee-deep in debt. But while a good argument can be made for going into debt in order to complete your education and achieve higher wages in your lifetime, I can't think of a single reason why you should rack up and carry credit-card debt.

When you have credit-card debt, the simple fact is that you'll pay approximately three times the cost of the item you purchased by the time you pay off the bill. The $200 boots you just had to have really will cost you $600, once you calculate the interest you'll pay on your debt. That $1,000 stereo system becomes a $3,000 investment. Your $2,500, five-day vacation to Bermuda will really cost you $7,500.

Here's how it works. Let's say you charge a $1,000 trip to Mexico on your credit card. The card charges you 1.5 percent per month, or 18 percent per year on the balance that you carry. That means you'll actually pay $1,180 for your trip to Mexico, assuming you pay it off at the end of a year. You might even pay a bit more. Typically, when you carry a balance, you are back-charged interest from the date of purchase (the free days are eliminated). Also, you are charged extra for the compounding of the interest and balance each month. Pay only the minimum each month, and your $1,000 trip can quickly rise to more than $3,000.

And we're talking *after-tax* dollars. That's the cash you bring home in your paycheck. If you're in the 28-percent tax bracket, you'll effectively have to earn close to $1.40 for every dollar you spend. You'll have to earn $840 to pay for your $200 boots that cost $600 after you pay off the credit card. You'll have to earn $4,200 to pay for your $1,000 stereo. And is that five-day vacation really worth $10,500? That's $2,100 per day, enough to pay for a suite in a five-star resort.

The faster you get rid of your credit-card debt, the sooner you can begin making the numbers work in your favor. One of the best ways to start is by paying off your credit card early. There are two ways to do this: consolidating your debt on a cheaper card, and prepaying your debt (see Simple Thing 16).

If you pay your bills on time, your credit ought to be fairly good, even if you have a large amount of debt. That means credit-card companies will be happy to extend special offers to you if you agree to consolidate your debt on their card.

Look carefully at the offer before you sign up. What you're doing is transferring the balance of your debt to a new card with a lower interest rate. You're looking to move down from a 16-percent (some cards charge more than 30 percent) interest rate to somewhere around 6 to 8 percent, or lower. Usually teaser rates are good for six months to a year. Try to find one that will last for a year. If you go shorter, be sure to keep your eyes open for another offer, since you'll need it soon. By continually shifting your credit-card debt to other credit cards with low teaser rates, and then adding all that extra monthly savings back into the check you send your credit-card company, you'll be getting ahead of the game.

If you currently own your own home and have equity in it, another way to consolidate your debt is to take out a home-equity loan or open a home-equity line of credit.

When you borrow against the cash you have in your home (referred to as your home's equity), you're getting a home-equity loan. The difference between a home-equity loan and a home-equity line of credit is how you receive the funds. With a loan, you typically receive all of your loan in a lump-sum payment. With a line of credit, you're given a checkbook (or, worse yet, another credit card) to use to draw against your line of credit.

A home-equity loan is nice because you get all of the cash at once, but you also start paying interest on the whole amount right away. With a home-equity line of credit, you get the cash as you need it, and pay interest as you borrow.

By using home-equity loan dollars to pay off your debt, you're accomplishing two things. First, the interest rate on a home-equity loan is frequently lower than that on a credit card. Introductory teaser rates on home-equity loans are often under 4 percent for the first six months (a rate you'll almost never find on a credit card), and regular rates start around the prime interest rate (the rate banks charge their best customers). In addition, if you itemize on your federal income tax form, you may deduct the interest you pay on a home-equity loan up to $100,000. Of course, if you take out a home-equity loan and do not change your spending habits, you'll be headed for bankruptcy.

Another way to go is to refinance your entire mortgage and take out cash. But you should only refinance if interest rates have dropped below the level of your current mortgage interest rate. Otherwise, getting a home-equity loan will probably be less expensive.

Although transferring your credit-card balance, taking out a home-equity loan, or opening up a home-equity line of credit can be time-consuming, if you can save thousands of dollars in credit-card interest payments, it's well worth it.

A GOOD START

If you're going to tap your home equity to pay off your credit-card debt, you need to make sure you're getting the best deal possible. Go to BankRate.com, an excellent financial services site with good articles about important personal finance topics. Search for the loan of your choice, and the site will give you several options.

You'll want to check out these companies, and then compare the costs to those costs and fees local lenders will charge you for a home-equity loan. Remember, your local bank or credit union may offer a home-equity loan as cheap as, or even cheaper than, one you can get on-line. You won't know until you check it out.

Also, it may be less expensive to get a new credit card, and take advantage of the six-month introductory rate, than to get a home-equity loan—even if you can deduct the interest. A home-equity loan might cost 9 percent. If you transfer the balance, you might only pay 2 to 3 percent for six months, at which point you'd have to transfer again. If you're vigilant about transferring the balance to a new low-interest card until the balance is paid off, it's less expensive to do that than to use a home-equity loan.

Here's how the math works. If you're in the 28-percent income tax bracket and you itemize, you're probably paying only 6.75 percent (true interest) on your home-equity loan after the deduction. That's pretty good, but nowhere near as good as 2 or 3 percent on a balance transfer.

Even though it's just a few percentage points, by now you know it all adds up to the creation of real wealth.

SIMPLE THING

16

PREPAY YOUR CREDIT-CARD DEBT

Once you transfer your credit-card balance to a new, lower-interest card, you should notice a significant drop in your monthly payments. Instead of paying only the new lower balance, continue to make the same monthly payments as before. This is called prepaying your credit-card debt. For example, let's say you owe $5,000 on your credit card, and that card is charging you 18 percent interest per year. The interest on the debt comes to $75 per month, and let's say your minimum payment due is $100 per month. If you transfer the debt to a card that is charging you only 6 percent interest, the monthly interest on the account is only $25 per month, so your minimum payment might fall to around $40 per month. You might first think, "Great, I'm saving $60 per month." And you are. But you can save more if you still pay $100 per month. That's because the extra $60 (plus $15 out of the $40 per month minimum) is used to pay down the balance of your loan. So (provided you don't charge anything new), the next month, your balance will be just $4,925, instead of $4,975.

When you prepay a loan (like a mortgage, home-equity loan, or credit-card debt), you're effectively earning a rate of return on your money equal to the net interest you're paying. So if your credit card has a 16-percent interest rate and you prepay that debt, every dollar you prepay effectively earns 16 percent. If your debt is carrying a 6-percent rate, your prepayment dollars effectively earn 6 percent.

When you factor in how compounding works, you end up saving the percentage rate you're being charged. But with a credit card, all of the savings comes at the end—in the form of not having to pay out the remaining years of the loan.

How fast should you prepay your credit-card debt? As fast as possible, and then some. In addition to putting every dollar you can toward your monthly credit-card payment, consider paying half of your bill every other week. What you're doing is actually making twenty-six semimonthly payments, or thirteen annual payments. If you're already adding an extra one-twelfth to each monthly payment, which is another way of adding in a thirteenth payment per year, you'll be adding a second thirteenth payment, which should cut your loan term virtually in half.

Because credit-card companies are required to credit your account shortly after they receive your funds, making two payments each month will boost your prepayment schedule significantly. And when you're fighting to pay down your debt as quickly as possible, you need every advantage you can get.

A GOOD START

If you're carrying a balance on your credit cards, and adding to it every month, you have to stop today. Take your cards and stick them in a bag with water and freeze them, give them to a trusted friend to hold, or cut them up. Now figure out how you're going to live on what you earn for the next month. Then find ways to save $100 or $200 per month. Take the cash and apply it directly toward your credit-card balance.

Although it may seem as though you'll never pay off your credit-card debt, it only takes a few months to see that you're really making a big dent. Paying down your account means you're being charged less interest each month. While the credit-card company may try to lower the minimum amount due (or even tell you that you can take a few months off), stick to the plan and contribute every dollar you can spare toward paying off the debt.

What works for your credit card will also work for your mortgage. Prepaying your mortgage can shorten the term of your loan by a decade or more, depending on how much you prepay.

Traditionally, if you make one extra mortgage payment per year (either in a lump sum or divided into twelve equal parts), you can shorten your thirty-year mortgage to about twenty-two years. If you make two extra payments per year, you can cut your thirty-year loan in half. All of those years that you don't have to make mortgage payments add up to tens or hundreds of thousands of dollars saved.

If you have a $100,000, thirty-year loan at 7 percent, you'll pay $139,510.98 in interest over the life of your loan. Your monthly payment will be about $665. If you pay an extra $50 per month, you'll shave six years off your loan and save more than $34,000. If you pay an extra $100 per month, you'll shave nearly ten years off your loan and save yourself more than $50,000 in interest.

Of course, the higher the interest rate, the more you'll save by prepaying your debt.

A word of caution about prepaying mortgages: It typically works best if you pick a set amount, like $50, $100, $150, or some other round figure, and enclose that amount in a separate check with your regular mortgage payment. It's easier to track and to figure out how much you're saving. Finally, you can prepay your mortgage all you like, but if you refinance or pay it all off and you have a prepayment penalty attached to your loan, you could owe as much as 3 or 4 percent of the loan amount as a penalty.

SIMPLE THING

17

CHOOSE A CREDIT CARD
THAT OFFERS SOMETHING
FOR NOTHING

If you can control your spending, and *if* you can pay off the balance each month, I don't see any reason why you shouldn't use a credit card for your daily expenses. It's easier for record-keeping purposes to get a checklist of your charges at the end of the month, and you may get such additional perks as insurance coverage when you rent a car or ship something from a store.

If you're in business for yourself, you'll need two cards; one for your business expenses and one for your house expenses.

But if you are going to make frequent use of a credit card, be savvy about it. Choose a card that gives you something for nothing (or almost nothing). For example, Discover will pay you up to 1 percent on everything you charge in cash. If you charge $25,000 over the course of a year, you'll receive a check for $225. Citibank will, for a small annual fee, give you one American Airlines mile for every dollar you charge. Bank One will give you a mile on United for every dollar your charge. If you fly either of these airlines frequently, you could earn enough between the two for a round-trip ticket each year. Other cards give you free gas, free miles on other airlines, or cash back on a car purchase.

Whichever freebie you choose, make sure you think it through. Don't get the card that gives you United miles if you fly American. And while miles are good, especially if you have to fly at a moment's notice and a next-day ticket costs $2,000, if you book ahead, you can fly almost anywhere in the U.S. for less than $300.

Don't get the card that gives you dollars toward a particular car if you haven't made up your mind which car (if any) you're likely to buy. You might just let your reward go to waste.

Finally, don't overpay for this privilege. Some cards require an annual payment of seventy-five dollars for an airline affiliate card that will give you one mile for every dollar you spend. But if you don't charge much each year and it takes you three years to earn a free ticket, you will have paid $225 in credit-card fees to get that "free" ticket. In that case you might have been better off had you gotten a cash-back card, planned ahead, and bought a discounted airplane ticket to the destination of your choice.

Try to find a card that gives you what you want with no annual fee. If you must pay an annual fee, try to keep it to twenty-five dollars (unless it's your business card and you can write off the annual fee). Keep focused on the goal: something for nothing.

A GOOD START

If you open up your wallet, you'll probably find at least four or five credit cards inside. You may have a gas card or two, a charge card from a local department store, and two major credit cards, like a Visa and MasterCard. You may even have others.

I recommend you carry only one or two credit cards in your wallet. One or two cards means you only need to worry about one or two statements each month, and you only have to keep track of two pieces of plastic. Careful use means that neither of the cards (or at least only one) will cost you anything. In the best case, both will give you back something, such as up to I percent cash back on your charges.

If you're in the market for a new credit card, go to BankRate.com and CardWeb.com to check out credit-card deals. You might also take a look at the dozens of credit-card solicitations you receive in the mail each year to see if there are any good offers.

Remember, don't apply for a new card (or any loan) unless you're absolutely sure you'll get approved. If you get rejected for a credit card, it can show up on your credit report and damage your credit history.

SIMPLE THING

18

CHECK YOUR CREDIT REPORT
AT LEAST ONCE A YEAR

We've all heard the horror story: Our mother, sister, brother, neighbor, or a friend of a friend goes to buy a house and finds out their credit stinks even though they've never reneged on a debt or paid a bill late.

Somewhere along the line, their credit history has been tampered with. Instead of a clean record, there is a huge medical bill outstanding, two charge-backs, or a defaulted lease on a Rolls-Royce. Perhaps their financial identity has been stolen and someone has applied for a dozen credit cards and racked up $200,000 in debt.

If there's going to be a happy ending to this story, it'll only come after a mountain of hard work. And don't even think about visiting a "credit repair" specialist. The only person who can improve your credit is you!

How do you avoid having problems with your credit history? You need to actively monitor your credit report. That means pulling a copy of your credit report each year and fixing any credit problems or errors that appear on it.

Here's what to do. First, order a credit report on yourself. Any of these three major national credit companies will sell you one:

Trans-Union (800-888-4213; Transunion.com)

Equifax (800-685-1111; Equifax.com)

Experian (888-Experian; Experian.com)

For less than ten dollars each (some states require credit reporting bureaus to give you one free copy per year of your credit report), these credit bureaus will send you your credit report. This is the same information that lenders and prospective creditors receive, and yet when you pull your credit report, it does not have a negative impact on it. (But if too many credit-card companies, car dealers, mortgage lenders, or stores pull copies of your credit report in too short a period of time, it can severely damage your credit history, even if you would otherwise have a "clean bill of health.")

By getting a copy of your credit report once a year (and certainly before you apply for a loan or another credit card), you'll get a first look at any problems, errors, or discrepancies that have sprung up. And then you can spring into action.

Fixing Problems

So let's say you've ordered your credit report from Trans-Union and it turns up an erroneous bill for twenty-five dollars from a doctor you've never heard of. You recognize this isn't your bill. What do you do?

Let's pause for a moment to consider how credit reporting bureaus like Trans-Union work. In our computerized, Big Brother–like world, credit bureaus generally have data exchange agreements with companies that provide credit: Visa, MasterCard, American Express, Discover, Diner's Club, other credit-card companies, department or retail stores, banks, credit unions, etc.

On a daily, weekly, monthly, or semiannual basis, these companies electronically send all of their information to the credit bureau, which stores it in a mammoth database and updates the records of each person on file. If you charge up a storm at the Gap and don't pay your Visa bill, it'll be noted on your credit report. If you apply for a credit card at Eddie Bauer, the store will pull a copy of your credit report and see if your credit score (think of it as your financial SAT) is high enough to be worthy of additional credit. Credit bureaus also list all debts and record information on whether you pay your taxes, are involved in a lawsuit, or if you have any court judgments against you.

Now that you know how credit bureaus work, here's how to fix a credit reporting problem. You should immediately notify the credit bureau (in writing, always in writing) that there are errors in your credit history. By law, the credit bureau must investigate the problem within thirty days.

You should also go directly to the source of a credit problem—the creditor. In the case of an erroneous doctor's bill, call the doctor's office and ask them to pull the invoice for the disputed bill. Work with the office to figure out whose bill it is. It's possible that a receptionist or billing assistant transposed two numbers in the patient's social security number. This will undoubtedly require many phone calls and other follow-ups, but make sure to get the resolution in writing.

When you can prove that a credit problem is not yours, the creditor should correct its computers. It may take some time, however, for that correction to work its way from a company's computer to your credit bureau. You can speed up the process by providing copies of the paperwork to the credit reporting bureau.

If you discover, during a routine review of your credit report, that someone else has been using your credit to purchase property, cars, furs, jewels, or any other items, you've got a huge problem. Immediately contact your attorney, your state's attorney general, and the nearest office of the Federal Trade Commission.

A GOOD START

One of the easiest scams to avoid is the credit-repair scam. Here's how it goes: You need help fixing your credit. For anywhere from $300 to $1,500, someone offers to wipe your credit history clean and get you started out with a blank slate.

Quite simply, it's a lie. No one can fix your credit as well as you can. And in all credit-repair cases, time is your friend, not your enemy.

The scam shapes up like this: If the credit repair company tells you they'll give you a new social security number, actually doing that is breaking the law. What they're really doing is applying for a Federal Employment Identification Number (FEIN), which has the same number of numerals as a social security number, and suggesting you use that to apply for a new credit line.

You're getting taken to the cleaners in several ways. First, by not using your real social security number at work, your wages aren't getting recorded to your real social security account. That means you could be shortchanged when you retire. Next, you may be paying for an illegal service—never a good idea. Finally, you are the only one who has the tools needed to really fix your credit history. You need to pay your bills on time and in full. And you have to let time go by.

If your finances are in such horrible shape that you need outside guidance, check out a local office of Consumer Credit Counseling Services (800-338-CCCS). You can get help budgeting and sorting out your finances for free. And unless you enroll in one of their workout programs (in which you pay them and they pay your creditors), it won't get reported on your credit history.

4

Investing Yourself in Your Investments

OPEN A BROKERAGE ACCOUNT

April is a very bright twenty-year-old who works full-time while putting herself through school full-time. She's paid off her credit-card debt and manages to save more than $200 per paycheck, which will amount to nearly $6,000 this year alone (not including what she's able to set aside in her company retirement plan).

She recently asked me if she should put her money into her savings account or invest it. It's money she intends to save and invest for a long-term expense, such as a down payment for a house or even for her retirement.

I suggested she open up a brokerage account at a financial institution, such as Charles Schwab or Fidelity Investments. Institutions like these (and there are many other fine ones) offer investors an easy way to manage and invest their money.

A brokerage account allows you to buy and sell equities, including shares of companies and mutual funds. You put your cash in a money-market account, only the interest rate is typically a bit better than at bank money-market accounts. When you buy a stock or shares in a mutual fund (either by calling the institution on the telephone or going online), the cash to pay for the trade is taken out of a core account and used to pay for your purchase. When you sell a stock, or shares in a mutual fund, the cash goes back into the core account.

Most institutions will allow you to write checks from your core account, and they'll give you the checkbook to do it. Sometimes there is a minimum amount, say $500 per check, or a limit on the number of checks you can write each month.

The benefit to having a brokerage account is that the funds are there when you're ready to make an investment. And while you wait, your money grows at a faster rate than in a traditional money-market account.

But a word of warning: Brokerage firms are not banks, and are not required to live by the rules and regulations that govern banks. Also, these accounts are not backed by the federal government. If you put up to $100,000 into a savings account at a local bank, those funds are most likely FDIC-insured, which means you'll get all of your money back should the bank fail. Brokerage firms don't have that kind of protection.

That's why you want to be extra careful when you select a brokerage company or financial institution. You want to find a company that's a leader in the field and is hugely successful. Although even the best companies can have financial troubles, you'll sleep better at night knowing you put your money into one of the biggest, best-known, and best-funded institutions.

A final thought: Once you've set up your brokerage account, it's easy to ask this company to withdraw twenty-five dollars, fifty dollars, or more from your paycheck automatically and direct-deposit it into your brokerage account. You'll probably never miss the money, and your savings will start to grow a whole lot faster.

A GOOD START

Before you plunk down your money into a brokerage account, you may want to fill in the gaps of your knowledge with a little reading. You'll get quite a bit of background from books like my *100 Questions You Should Ask About Your Personal Finances*, but there are places to go for information as well.

The Internet has excellent information. Web sites like Fool.com (Motley Fool), CNBC.com, BankRate.com, CBSMarketwatch.com, and Quicken.com give you general, independent information. Morningstar.com is an excellent resource for mutual-fund information. Major firms like Merrill Lynch, Fidelity Investments, Charles Schwab, and Vanguard have well-done Web sites loaded with detailed investing information.

Financial magazines, available at your local library, are a good, general source of information. My favorite ones are *Money, Smart Money,* and *Worth.* While you're at the library, you may want to take a look at *The Wall Street Journal,* the business section of *The New York Times,* and *Investor's Business Daily.* While these publications may seem complicated when you first start reading them, you'll quickly catch on and soon find they contain interesting and useful bits of knowledge.

SIMPLE THING
20

TAKE ENOUGH RISK

When it comes to investing, the longer you have, the more risk you should take. That sounds easy (and perhaps even intuitive), but many individuals see risk-taking as something to be avoided at all costs.

Unfortunately, if you don't take enough risk, you run the very real risk of running out of cash during your retirement years. A child born after the year 2000 has an increasing chance of living one hundred years. That could mean as much as thirty-five to forty years in retirement! To get you through those years comfortably (will you really want to work when you're ninety-nine?), you'll need to take enough risk to power your financial life.

There are four factors you should consider when thinking about your investments and how much risk you're willing to take:

Risk Factor No. 1: Age

If you believe the ads on TV, you can beat the effects of aging by taking herbs, working out with the hot personality or machine of the week, rubbing cream on your cellulite, or having various surgeries to tuck and smooth what nature has wrought. But you don't want to shortcut the process of time when it comes to your investments. In fact, you want every second to work its magic on your money.

Your age should have an impact on what you do with your money, because your age generally correlates with a particular stage in life. For example, if you're at age fifty and hope to retire by seventy, you have a twenty-year period to salt away retirement funds while you're still working. But even with that kind of time line, you may not take as much risk as a thirty-year-old couple who have twenty years to invest for their children's college tuition. (Remember, your child can get a loan or scholarship to attend school, but no one will lend you a dime for your retirement.)

Risk Factor No. 2: Health

If you have a serious illness, no matter what your age, you might make a very different decision about how to invest your cash than you would if your health weren't an issue. For example, if you need cash today to pay for medical bills or a long-term-care facility, you might liquidate your life insurance, sell investments, or use up your 401(k), even if it meant paying an IRS penalty on top of the income taxes.

You might not put money in an investment like high-tech growth stocks that require ten years to ride out the volatility in this market sector. Instead, you might choose to invest in tax-free municipal bonds that pay dividends.

Risk Factor No. 3: Wealth

If you're already wealthy, you can afford to risk more of your wealth for a longer period. That's because if you lose a portion of your assets, it will hurt you less than it would someone who doesn't have that kind of money.

You can also participate in higher-risk, higher-reward investments, such as hedge funds, which require a substantial net worth but can return as much as 30 to 100 percent annually. You might also want to trade on margin (which means borrowing against assets to invest in other equities)—a risky endeavor, to be sure, but doable if you have the cash to cover a margin call (for repayment) should the market take a sudden dive.

The bottom line is, when you have a certain amount of funds (and the number is different for everyone), you can afford to take more risk.

Risk Factor No. 4: Taxes

If your goal is to defer taxes, or to pay as little as possible, you may want to buy stock in high-growth companies that pay little (if anything) in the way of dividends and instead reinvest all of the cash in growing the company. You'll take more risk (particularly if you invest in only a couple of different companies), but you'll be better able to control your capital gains, the profit you make on the sale of the stock.

On the other hand, if you're risk-averse but want to accomplish the same goal, you might instead invest in tax-free municipal bonds.

Balancing Risk

Although you can take more risk by investing in international companies or fast-growing sectors like technology and biotechnology, you can balance the risk by diversifying into investments that offer a different sort of risk and move out of step with your other investments. For example, you can invest part of your assets in bonds instead of putting 100 percent of your money into the stock market. Or you can diversify your stock holdings by splitting up funds into different sectors, such as energy, technology, commodities, and utilities.

A GOOD START

It's one thing to take a measured risk when you fully understand what you're doing. It's quite another to increase your risk by engaging in risky behavior. Here are some things you can do to make sure the risk you take will still let you sleep at night:

- Don't buy or sell stock without a good reason.
- Stick with your investment strategy, but make sure you change it to suit the major changes in your life.
- Be realistic about what the market can do for your finances.
- Don't let your emotions drive investment decisions.
- Regularly reevaluate your investment returns.
- Don't invest money in extremely risky investments if you can't afford to lose it.
- Do your homework. Choosing solid investments isn't brain surgery, but it won't come to you by osmosis, either.
- Don't get greedy. The old saying on Wall Street is "Pigs get fat. Hogs get slaughtered."

SIMPLE THING

21

CHOOSE INVESTMENTS
THAT YOU UNDERSTAND

So much money is lost by people who think they understand an investment—and don't. The most successful investors are the ones who keep it simple: Don't invest in anything you can't explain to a ten-year-old.

But to avoid making this mistake, take a moment to consider why we invest in things we don't understand. Often it's because we think we're too stupid to understand how to invest our money. We have this self-esteem problem because it's in the financial industry's best interest to make consumers feel as though they need an investment expert or all will be lost.

Of course, reality is quite different from advertising. While some stock brokers have master's degrees in business administration (MBAs), others, many of whom work for large investment companies, started off flipping burgers at a local fast-food joint. Or they taught school, worked as salespeople in retail department stores, or stayed home and raised their kids before their leap into high finance.

Anyway, the way many brokers operate is to call you up on the phone (at dinnertime, of course!) and invite you to partake in one of the hottest investments this century will ever see! Or perhaps you've already got an investment adviser and you read an article about margin trading and said, "I'd like to give that a try."

You have to be about as lucky as a lottery winner (or Hillary Clinton) to make money your first time out buying options or futures or buying on margin. Instead, it's often a disaster.

When I was writing this book, I received a letter from a reader who was concerned about her brother. He had a stay-at-home wife and three daughters. He owned his home and earned $45,000 per year. That was the good news. Unfortunately, he'd taken out a $45,000 second mortgage and lost it all trading options. He then charged up another $45,000 on his credit cards and lost that in the stock market as well. And while his property value had risen a little bit, it was nowhere near enough to pay off even the $45,000 home-equity loan on his house.

For this family, which has more than $180,000 in debt (the $90,000 in the home-equity loan plus the credit-card debt, in addition to a $90,000 first mortgage on a house worth perhaps $135,000), bankruptcy may be the only option. It's a bitter lesson. The sister mentioned that she didn't think her brother completely understood what he was investing in. He also probably didn't realize that his investment mistakes could cost him his family home.

Anyone can get lucky in gambling. But when you invest in something you don't understand, you might as well be throwing dice in a Las Vegas craps game.

A GOOD START

Once you've read up on an investing concept, turn around and try to explain it to your spouse or partner. For example, have your spouse or partner ask you what a mutual fund is. (A mutual fund invests in a group of publicly traded companies.)

It's helpful to explain these things aloud because you'll find out which concepts you're fuzzy on, and you can read up on them. With practice, you'll soon be able to explain all sorts of investment vehicles to everyone.

DON'T TAKE HOT TIPS
FROM A COLD CALL

You've just prepared a great meal, called in the kids, had everyone sit down, and are passing around the food when the phone rings. It's a stockbroker cold-calling you about this week's great stock that you just can't live without owning.

Taking hot tips from a cold call is about the worst thing you can do when it comes to investing. Really, if this company was such a hot tip, why is this stockbroker calling you instead of his mother?

The truth is, taking stock tips from anyone (brokers, relatives, your doctor, best friend, or the neighborhood barber) is a really bad idea. Unless people are intimately involved with the company they're recommending, chances are they don't know what's going on. (And if they are intimately involved with a company and you trade on their tips, you could get indicted for "insider trading.")

When I talk about avoiding hot tips from cold calls, it also applies to sweepstakes (do you know anyone who actually won $10 million?), promotions, giveaways, or any other contest that promises you something if only you'll purchase a twenty-five dollar subscription to a magazine you'll never read.

And watch out for money-management magazines when they run headlines proclaiming "Top 10 Stocks to Buy

Before the End of the Year." These stories have a lead time of three to four months; that means they're written and edited up to four months before the magazine goes to print. A lot can change in that time. (Although some of the money magazines I consider to be top-rated—*Smart Money*, *Money*, and *Worth*—get it on the nose from time to time, read these magazines for the basic how-to articles, and take these stock-picking articles with a grain of salt.)

So when should you take a hot tip from a cold call? Never. Even if it means you miss the deal of a lifetime, the odds aren't in your favor. For every time you make money with a hot tip, you might lose money the next one hundred times.

A GOOD START

Turn off the ringer at dinner. Anyone you want to talk to will leave a message or call back. Nothing else is worth interrupting dinner.

If you do happen to pick up a cold call, simply interrupt the caller and say clearly, "Please take this number off your lists." If the caller persists, say it again and add "The FTC requires your company to remove my name from your lists when asked. Please do so, or I will report your company." Removing your name can take five to six weeks.

SIMPLE THING

23

DON'T PUT ALL YOUR EGGS
IN ONE BASKET

Back when a farmer would collect fresh eggs and put them in a wire or wicker basket to carry them back to the house, he took a risk that if the basket fell, some or all of the eggs would break. Because selling eggs was fairly profitable, and hens laid only so many eggs a day, the risk of losing some of that profit was real and sizable.

Hence the old saw: Don't put all your eggs in one basket. If you put a few eggs into several baskets, you're lowering the risk that you'll trip on the way back from the henhouse two or three times, and break all of your eggs.

In the investment world, this same advice applies. When someone says, "Don't put all of your eggs in one basket," they're trying to tell you to diversify your financial portfolio because the risk of holding everything in the same place is huge compared to the profit you may or may not make.

Employees of high-tech companies in the late 1980s and 1990s might disagree with me, since many of them walked away from companies like Microsoft, Intel, or Sun Microsystems as multimillionaires. They got that way because the company gave them stock options early on, and several years later the stock price went through the stratosphere. But what if you placed all your assets in your company stock and the stock price didn't move for ten years, as was the case with IBM? Or, if you joined Microsoft and the company's stock dived 50 percent, as it did in the year 2000? Keeping all your investment eggs in that basket meant you lost out on profits you would have made if your portfolio had been spread out among other companies, industries, or market sectors. You may have even lost some or all of your principal.

Experts generally say that if you buy stock in individual companies, you should keep no more than 10 to 15 percent of your total assets in any one company. So if your assets (excluding your house) are worth $50,000, you should keep no more than $5,000 to $7,500 in the stock of any one company. If that company's stock goes up significantly, you'll need to rebalance your portfolio by selling some of the stock in that company.

If you purchase mutual funds, you're already diversifying your basket of eggs because traditional mutual funds never hold more than 5 percent of their assets in any single stock, and may actually hold positions in as many as 400 companies.

In investing, keeping all your investment eggs in one basket is akin to playing the lottery. If you win, you win big. But the odds of winning are about 12,000 (or the current number of companies listed on the U.S. stock market) to one.

A GOOD START

A television producer recently asked me what she should do with all of her company-owned stock. "Right now, whenever I reach $5,000 in stock, I sell half of it and purchase something else." I think she's doing the right thing. Even if the stock of the company for which you work is doing beautifully, it may hit a rough spot down the line.

By selling the stock a little at a time and diversifying into other investments, you're spreading your risk. You may make less overall, but in the end you'll likely lose a whole lot less in a severe market downturn.

So consider selling a portion of your company stock on a regular basis. Try not to have any one company represent more than 10 to 15 percent of your total investment pie. If nothing else, you'll certainly sleep better at night.

SIMPLE THING

24

TAKE RESPONSIBILITY FOR YOUR INVESTMENTS

Did someone hold a gun to your head when you made your last investment? The answer, almost certainly, is no. So why are you blaming everyone else because the investment didn't do as well as you had hoped?

The truth is, it's a lot easier to take a hot tip from a cold call (or get one by the water cooler) than to go out and do your own research. Doing your own research requires spending time to read about a particular company, investigating what products it makes or what services it performs, thinking about your investment strategy and how this particular investment works within it, and evaluating whether or not this is the right time (not to mention the right price) to buy into this investment.

Taking responsibility for your investments means you have to act like a grownup. You need to know what you have, what you owe, and what financial goals you're trying to achieve. You must avoid becoming emotionally involved with your investments, so that when the time comes to sell (and you'll always reach that point), you'll be able to make as objective a decision as possible.

Taking responsibility means being a doer, not a procrastinator. It means teaching yourself what you don't know and finding the right professionals to help you when you're out of your depth. It also means not blaming anyone else for your procrastination, lack of research, or mistakes. The flip side is stellar: When you do your research and everything goes according to plan, you'll have earned the accolades yourself.

A GOOD START

Buy a small, spiral-bound notebook. Date it the day you purchase it. This is going to be the place in which you jot down your daily financial doings. You can write your daily expenses in it, but also keep track of whatever you do that relates directly to your personal finance. It might be research into a company, or it might simply be spending an hour at the library paging through money magazines. It might be that you entered the week's receipts into your financial software.

Whatever you do that day, write it down. Keep track by date, and try to do something every day. The idea is that soon managing your money will be like putting on a pair of shoes—something you do almost every day.

5

Big Purchases:
Cars, Homes, College
Tuition, and Weddings

NEVER LEASE A CAR

When I was writing *100 Questions You Should Ask About Your Personal Finances*, I spent several months researching the world of cars and trucks. After interviewing dozens of dealers, consumers, consumer advocates, and government officials, I came to two conclusions: Never lease a car, and always buy a used car rather than a new one.

The problem with leasing is that you'll pay on a car forever, and still wind up not owning anything. Leases are expensive, convoluted, and difficult to calculate, especially since the law doesn't require dealers to disclose all of the numbers. And it's easy for less honorable dealers to slip items into the contract that you didn't agree to.

I don't get the supposed "financial benefits" of leasing a car. To me, it's a little like renting an apartment. Basically, when you rent an apartment, you're paying someone else's mortgage. When you lease a car, you're paying the car loan for the dealer. When you turn the car back in, you're charged for any excess mileage driven and any dents and bruises that the dealer deems to be "out of the ordinary."

A GOOD START

The easy solution is to simply buy your car. Get preapproved for a car loan from your lender of choice ahead of time (your credit union is typically a good, relatively inexpensive place to start). Then shop around to price out the model in which you're interested.

When you buy a car, your monthly payments will go toward building up equity. When you're done making the payments, you'll own your car free and clear. At that time you can decide if you want to keep the car, or trade it in for another one. If you buy a new car and keep it for ten years, studies have shown that you'll be thousands of dollars richer in retirement.

WHEN IT COMES TO CARS, BUY USED, NOT NEW

Having owned my Honda for nearly seven years, I have to agree that there's nothing nicer than getting into a new vehicle. And every time I rent a car, it feels great. No crumbs on the floor or stains on the floor mat. No kiddie car seats making imprints on new backseats. And the outside is so shiny I can almost see my face in the hood.

And then I think about how the brand-new car looked after it spent a week with my family—just like my old Honda in our garage!

It's not that I have anything against new cars, except they don't do a darned thing to help your finances. The day you drive your brand new car off the lot, its value drops by as much as 25 percent. That new-car smell is really the smell of money going right out the window!

So if you really need a set of wheels, consider buying a used car. Buying used means the depreciation comes out of someone else's pocket, not yours. The loss of value in a car is far less steep from years three to six than from years one to three, which means you'll keep more of your dollars when the time comes for you to sell the car.

If you like fancy cars, but can't afford to drop $30,000 to $50,000 on a new Cadillac, a Lexus, or an Infiniti, buying a used car is one way to drive what you like without paying full freight. For example, a new Infiniti with all the trimmings might cost you $50,000. Three years later you might find one for between $30,000 and $35,000. If you look carefully, you'll find one that's barely been driven and has been taken care of properly.

When you buy a used car ("pre-owned" is the fancy term you'll hear these days), make sure you buy one that's still under factory warranty. Many dealers will "dealer certify" pre-owned cars and, for a small amount of cash, perhaps $100–$200, extend the life of the original warranty. Read the fine print, but this can be a good option.

You can buy a used car from an individual or from the dealer. If you buy directly from the owner, you're likely to save a few extra bucks. Choose this option only if you know the owner personally (and how they used or abused the car) or if you know something about cars and aren't afraid to negotiate directly with a person rather than an institution.

But there's nothing wrong with going through a dealer. Dealerships today are filled to the gills with cars coming off a two-, three-, or four-year lease. Just make sure you choose a dealer with a good reputation.

Before you do any negotiating whatsoever, you'll want to know the make, model, performance history, and blue-book price (its current value) of the car in which you're interested. *Consumer Reports* (or its Web site) is a good place to start. Once you get the background information on the car you want, and have located a pre-owned version of the car, get your financing in order.

Dealer financing is typically expensive. In fact, a new study showed that dealers will often add a couple of percentage points to the car loan (without the owner's approval) to pad their profit. You don't need the hassle of dealer financing, and over time you'll save hundreds or thousands of dollars if you line up your financing separately, before you go in to negotiate with the dealer.

As we've discussed, good places to check for auto loans include your local credit union, bank (you might even decide to get a home-equity loan, a less expensive alternative, especially if you can write off the interest), or large financing sites on the Internet. Start at BankRate.com, which will offer the most current rate and pricing information.

A GOOD START

Start your search for a slightly-used car by asking your friends and relatives (who take care of their cars) if they, or someone they know, plan on getting rid of their car anytime soon. You'll want to start this process at least six to nine months ahead of the time you need to purchase your new car. See if you can find a consensus on which local dealerships are the most reputable. If you ask around, you may find an excellent car at an advantageous price.

As for negotiating the price of the car, you'll need to shop around and do your homework. Know the blue-book value going in, and the price you'll pay at all of the car dealers in the area. Know the value of the amenities and options the car has (like air-conditioning, a CD player, or leather seats) and what a few dings and dents might do to the price tag.

Finally, the best piece of advice I can give you is this: Be ready to walk away if you don't get your price. There's always another car.

SET UP A HOUSE FUND

If buying a home is at the top of your list of financial goals, you'll need to get your budget and finances in shape. That means setting aside enough money to pay your bills, set up an emergency fund, and then some.

Some folks put all of their extra cash into a general savings account. The problem with doing it that way is that it's too easy to start spending the house money on groceries. By creating a separate fund for your house money, and putting it in a place that's perhaps a little less convenient to get to, you'll view this account as untouchable. It's your proverbial nest egg.

Let's call this separate pool of money your house fund. This should be the place you put every available nickel toward the down payment, closing costs, and moving expenses associated with buying a home. To get the maximum return while taking the smallest amount of risk, consider putting the money in a money-market account or a certificate of deposit (CD) at your local bank.

How much do you need to save? Today, you can get a mortgage with nothing down and finance up to 3 percent of your closing costs. If you get a zero-down mortgage, you'll need to save up for your moving costs. A recent study indicated that home buyers spend about $9,000 in moving and related expenses when buying a new home.

But let's assume you're going to put down 3 percent of the sales price of the home, plus another 3 percent of the mortgage amount for closing costs and fees. On a $100,000 house, you'll need $3,000 for the down payment, and about $2,800 in closing costs and fees. Figure another $3,000 to $6,000 for moving expenses and you're looking at nearly $9,000 to $12,000 in cash. Ouch!

If that seems like all of the money in the world, it's not. There are plenty of things you can do to save that kind of money in a year or two. But it requires adhering to your budget and occasionally doing without some luxury good or item.

Earlier in the book (Simple Thing 7), I gave you ten suggestions on ways to save money, including not buying junk food, buying your groceries in bulk, purchasing all your insurance policies from the same company, adjusting your thermostat, bringing your food from home, buying a used car, renting a movie (rather than going out to the movies), cooking at home, taking public transportation, changing local and long-distance telephone companies, and kicking a bad habit.

In Simple Thing 8, we looked at how much money you'd save by giving up that bad habit. Giving up a pack of cigarettes a day will net you about $1,460 over a year. Giving up a daily cup of gourmet coffee will allow you to keep another $1,000 per year. These two things alone, besides improving your health, will get you halfway to home ownership. Saving your change (and the lowest denomination bill) should net you another $1,000 to $2,000 per year.

Add up these savings and any gifts you may receive in the year, and pretty soon you'll be shopping for a home loan.

A GOOD START

Here are ten other ways to save money:

1. Buy jeans, T-shirts, and other staples at discount stores, or tag sales.

2. Do free things with your kids on weekends, like bike riding, walking, or playing games at home instead of going out to the movies.

3. Do your own maintenance work around the house, including painting (I draw the line at cleaning the gutters, unless you have a ranch home).

4. Seed your lawn instead of using sod (the cost is pennies per square foot versus three dollars or more per square foot for sod).

5. Send in rebate coupons for cash.

6. Only use ATMs that are in your bank's network and don't charge a fee.

7. Plan vacations well in advance, in order to take advantage of periodic airfare "wars."

8. Buy magazines with an annual subscription instead of off the shelf, or read them for free at the library.

9. Borrow books from the library instead of buying them, or buy paperback instead of hardcover books.

10. Don't settle for less. Do without until you can afford to buy what you really want.

Being conscious of where your cash goes is a way to exert positive control in your life. As you add other money-saving measures to your budget, earmark these savings for your house fund. Set a goal that you'll have enough cash for your down payment and closing costs within two years, and you'll find you're there before you know it.

BUY THE SMALLEST, CHEAPEST HOUSE ON A VERY GOOD BLOCK IN THE BEST SCHOOL DISTRICT YOU CAN AFFORD

When you're purchasing something relatively inexpensive, like groceries, underwear, or even lightbulbs, it's easy to shop around and find the best deal. After all, an orange is an orange, and a package of Hanes briefs is the same no matter whether you buy it at your local department store or Wal-Mart.

It's even easy to price-shop for a bigger item, like a car. You can go online or contact an organization like Consumer Reports and find out what the dealer paid for the car, and then price-shop until you find a dealer willing to give it to you for the price you want to pay.

But when it comes to buying a house, it's difficult to shop around for the best deal. Why? Every house is different. And if that weren't tough enough, market conditions can change on a whim.

If the market is tight, and there aren't enough homes for all of the buyers who want them, you could find yourself bidding against a dozen other home buyers for the same property. That's just going to drive prices up. If the market is slow, and there are more homes than interested buyers, prices will fall. And when prices have risen dramatically over a long period of time, you may well wonder when those prices are going to come down. Those unfortunate home buyers who bought at the top of the market in Southern California or New England in 1988 woke up in 1989 to find their property had lost half its value. (It would be a decade before some properties reached those values once again.)

So how do you protect yourself?

1. **Buy a home in a great school district.** Many studies have shown that homes located in excellent school districts tend to appreciate faster than homes located in mediocre or poor school districts. Whether or not you have kids, these neighborhoods are a better bet for home appreciation.

2. **Look for a good neighborhood with lots of homes in good condition that are in your price range or a bit higher, shopping, transportation options, and a variety of recreational activities.** Fortunately, good school districts tend to have good neighborhoods.

3. **Buy the smallest home on the best block, not the largest home on the worst block.** If you can't afford the home of your dreams in the neighborhood of your dreams, it's often better to buy a smaller home that you can fix up in your dream neighborhood. If you find a small home on a block with bigger homes, and the small house has the same size lot, you'll probably be able to expand the house later as your income and budget expands. (Before you buy, check to make sure you don't run into future zoning problems with your local planning department.)

4. **Buy a fixer-upper.** The best way to build in value is to fix up a home in a neighborhood where most of the other homes are already fixed up and selling at a

premium. Every day people buy a home for, say, $150,000 on a block of $400,000 homes, spend another $150,000 to fix it up, and end up with a profit of $100,000.

So if you're looking for a house, buy the smallest, least-fixed-up house on a very good block in the best school district you can afford. It's a sure-fire recipe for success!

(For more detailed information on how to buy a home, take a look at another of my books, *100 Questions Every First-Time Home Buyer Should Ask*.)

A GOOD START

One of the neat things about home ownership is that you not only get to live in your home, but it usually goes up in value. Since homes located in a good school district appreciate at a far faster rate than homes in a mediocre or poor school district, you'll want to start your search by figuring out which schools are rated the highest.

Start by looking up various school districts to see how they compare. This is easiest to do by tapping into such Web sites as SchoolMatch.com. You can also go to the government "blue pages" of your Yellow Pages and contact the state education department. For a few dollars, you can get a school-by-school breakdown of various criteria for your county. Some of this information may be available online. Once you've identified certain school districts, you'll want to spend time in those neighborhoods to figure out which best meets your needs.

BE A LANDLORD

If you can't afford to buy even a small house in your dream neighborhood, don't despair. You can still become a home-owner. It's just that you may have to consider owning a house or building with two or more units instead of a single-family home.

Purchasing a multi-unit apartment building (with four units or less) or a two-flat allows you to offset some of the expense of the mortgage with the rental income you receive. If you do it right, you could end up living for free or close to it.

Several years ago, Bob bought a Washington, D.C., townhouse with three bedrooms and two baths. He rented each of the bedrooms out to his friends and built a fourth bedroom and bathroom in the walk-out basement for himself. The rent he receives more than pays for his mortgage, real-estate taxes, and insurance. He's happy because he lives for free, and his friends are happy because they pay below-market rent in one of the nation's most expensive rental markets.

But you can make this strategy work for you wherever you live. Look around for a multi-unit building in a neighborhood you like and can afford. Work with a lender who can tell you how much you can afford to spend. It will be more than what you can afford on your salary, since lenders will give you a credit for 75 percent of the rental dollars that the rental unit is already generating.

One of the best parts of buying a multi-unit building instead of a single-family home is that it often turns into a working asset for you, once you've decided you're ready financially to buy another home. It may be possible for you to rent out the unit in which you've been living and have that bring in enough income to make the building pay for itself and then some.

What you've done then is to create an income-producing asset that is being paid for with other people's money. One day, your mortgage will be paid off and all of the rental income will be extra income for you.

A GOOD START

Look around in your neighborhood for other kinds of living arrangements. Specifically, you're looking for two-, three-, and four-apartment buildings. Then you need to investigate how much they cost and if your budget (remember, you'll get some credit with your lender for rental income) will permit you to purchase one. If your neighborhood of choice doesn't offer these sorts of buildings, you may have to expand your search into neighborhoods that do.

Next, check in with a mortgage lender who can help you figure out how large a mortgage you can afford if you purchase a two-, three-, or four-family home to live in and rent out.

SIMPLE THING
30

GET SMART ABOUT
YOUR FINANCING

It isn't enough to buy the best property in the best location at the best price if you waste money on your financing. The same thing is true about buying a car, boat, or motorcycle, or making any other large purchase. It's terrific if you shop around for the item, but if you don't shop around for the financing, you could wind up wasting hundreds or thousands of dollars.

If you can't pay cash (and who *can* pay cash for these large investments?), then you have to get smart about how you borrow the cash you need. Doing it the easy way often means you're paying a lot more than you have to.

For example, there are several ways to finance the purchase of a car: You can get financing from the dealer (most expensive, unless the dealer is offering factory incentives and rebates, such as 1.9-percent financing), or you can line up your own financing ahead of time. If you're going to line up your own financing, you can either take out a home-equity loan (if you own your own home and have equity available in it), go to several local lenders, like your local bank, or go online and price-shop.

When it comes to financing a house, the same rules apply. You can ask the seller to finance you (typically the least expensive way to go), look online, or check with local mortgage brokers and bankers.

Make sure you get a loan that meets your needs. For example, if you're going to live in your home for only five years or less, there's no reason to waste money on a thirty-year mortgage. You'll pay less with a five-year adjustable-rate loan or a five-year balloon loan (a loan in which you pay interest and principal for a set number of years, such as five or seven, at which time the entire remaining loan balance comes due at once).

With a car, you'll want to get no more than a three- or four-year loan. Every extra year of loan length adds hundreds of dollars in interest to the price of the car. If you get a five-year loan, pay extra each month so that you can pay off the loan in less time (without paying a prepayment penalty).

Unless you're planning to hold on to your home (or keep the mortgage) for thirty years, or something close to that, there's no need to choose a thirty-year loan to finance your purchase. With a thirty-year loan, you're paying for stability in the loan rate that you don't need if you're only going to stay five to seven years.

So be sure to consider an adjustable-rate mortgage (ARM), a two-step loan, or even a fifteen-year fixed-rate mortgage. Not only will you be making a good investment, but you'll be saving money as you pay for it as well.

A GOOD START

When shopping for a loan, you need to take into account all of the points (a point is one percent of the loan amount), costs, and fees, in addition to the interest rate. Generally, seller financing will be the cheapest kind, since sellers don't usually charge any fees or points, other than the cost of getting a copy of your credit report.

Credit unions tend to be cheaper than banks or other kind of lenders. Conventional lenders are pretty much in the same category for mortgages, since that market is so competitive (watch out for a lender who appears to offer a rate that's way below the market). Mortgage brokers typically deal with a handful of investors, and a legitimate mortgage broker may be able to find you a great deal.

For cars, banks and credit unions will be far cheaper than dealer financing (unless there's a special deal going on, as we discussed earlier). Make sure you have your financing lined up ahead of time so you don't have to take an expensive deal at the last minute.

PREPAY YOUR HOME LOAN

As we discussed in Simple Thing 16, paying off your credit card twice a month instead of only once a month is a smart move. Also, making a thirteenth payment per year, or an additional one-twelfth payment added to each check, will shave months or years off of your credit-card repayment plan.

The same prepayment principles work for a mortgage. And because the number is so much bigger (hopefully!) than your credit-card bills, the benefits to prepayment are that much larger.

Here's how it works: If you have a thirty-year loan and you make one extra payment per year, it will shave nine years off the length of your loan term. In other words, you'll be done paying off your thirty-year loan in just twenty-one years. If you make two extra payments per year, you'll cut your loan to about fifteen years.

Let's assume you have a $100,000 mortgage at 8 percent. You'll pay about $8,808 in interest and principal each year, with a monthly interest and principal payment of about $734. If you make one extra payment per year on a thirty-year fixed-rate loan, you'll shave nine years off the length of your loan. In other words, you'll pay off your home loan in twenty-one years and save approximately $79,270. To get that savings, you will have paid around $15,000 before you had to (you'd have owed it anyway, and then some). That's a pretty good return on your investment.

I'm often asked how prepaying works if you have a fifteen-year mortgage. The answer is not as well as with a thirty-year loan. That's because there is a lot less time for the interest to compound with a fifteen-year loan than with a thirty-year loan. And compounding is how prepayment works its magic.

Imagine a bank account with $1,000 in it. If the bank is paying you 4 percent simple interest on your money, the first year you'd end up with $1,040. The second year you'd end up with $1,081.60. The third year you'd end up with $1,124.68. The fourth year you'd end up with $1,169.86, and so on. Because you're earning interest on the interest, your money grows that much faster.

A mortgage works in reverse. As you pay down a few dollars of principal each month, the interest on the loan is smaller. But you're paying so little in principal and so much in interest that at the end of the first year you may have paid off only $1,000 in principal on a $100,000 loan. Over the rest of the loan term, the principal part of your monthly payment gets progressively bigger and the interest gets progressively smaller. In the thirtieth year of your loan, the position is reversed from year one: almost every dollar of your monthly payment is principal and the rest is interest.

If you prepay the principal on your loan, you're paying the loan from the back end, which is how the years get shaved off the loan term. Because what you're saving is the interest on that money, compounded through the years remaining on your loan term, you get a big bang for your buck.

With a fifteen-year loan, you're already saving those fifteen years of interest and more for the thirty-year loan. I say "more" because the average interest rate on a fifteen-year loan is usually less than on a thirty-year loan. For example, if the rate on a thirty-year fixed rate loan is 7.75 percent, the rate on a fifteen-year mortgage might be 7.5 percent, a savings of a quarter percent. (That may not sound like a lot, but you're saving a quarter percent on the entire loan amount, which can be thousands of dollars over the life of a loan.)

If you make one extra payment per year on a fifteen-year loan, you'll cut the loan from fifteen years to approximately eleven and a half years. Imagine that—you can pay off your mortgage in just over eleven years.

Before you start to ask, no, it's not better for you to keep the higher debt and prepay it. Any way you look at it, it's still cash out of pocket. You're better off using your monthly "savings" to prepay your debt and save thousands of dollars in interest over the life of the loan.

If you get a low down-payment loan and have to pay private mortgage insurance (equal to .4 to .6 percent of the loan amount per year), you'll have to keep making those payments until you have at least 20 percent equity in your home. Once you drop the private mortgage insurance, or PMI, you'll save maybe $100 per month. If you keep paying the $100 per month extra each month, which you're already programmed to do, you'll end up shaving years off the life of your loan, saving yourself thousands more than you'd have paid into the mortgage.

Once you buy a home, you'll undoubtedly receive offers to make your payments bimonthly. Lenders will offer (usually for a fee of $250 to $500) to set up an account that will process your payment twice a month, shaving more time off your loan. Essentially, paying twice a month equals a thirteenth payment or putting an extra one-twelfth in with your monthly mortgage payment.

Don't get suckered in. Whether you make a single additional thirteenth payment per year, or break it up into additional one-twelfth payments, or even send it twice a month to the mortgage company, there's no need for you to pay anyone extra to do this for you. Instead, save the cash and send that in with your next mortgage payment.

If you're going to prepay your loan, make sure you keep the level of prepayment at the same amount each month for at least a year. It's easier for your lender to lose track of payments or miscalculate how much extra you've sent in if you vary the extra amount each month.

Also, make sure you keep track of your additional payments. That way you'll create a record you can check against what the bank is telling you.

A GOOD START

Some loans carry "prepayment penalties." Such a penalty tries to catch people by charging them an exorbitant amount of money if they refinance or otherwise pay off their loan within the first two to four years. Some loans have prepayment penalties that are in effect for up to six years.

When you apply for a mortgage, you have to read the fine print. Make sure your loan allows you to prepay. Most loans allow you to make an extra mortgage payment or two anytime during the loan term, as long as you do not pay off the loan before the prescribed time. Other loans limit the amount you can prepay. If you think you may sell your home and pay off your loan, or refinance your loan, before the prepayment penalty period is up, avoid loans with prepayment penalties.

SIMPLE THING
32

MAINTAIN YOUR HOUSE
AND LANDSCAPING

If you think the cash out flow stops once you buy your home, you're probably not quite prepared for home ownership.

Depending on the type of house you have, you'll spend a fair amount each year maintaining it or improving its condition. Why? Materials wear out, paint wears off, parts break, and sewer lines often clog with tree roots. If you have a brick house and don't tuck-point the brick every fifteen years or so, you could get moisture leaking through the brick and rotting out the interior of your house. If you don't fix the leak in your roof, you could wind up with rotting roof timbers. If you don't unclog your sewer lines, you may have raw sewage backing up into your basement.

Although maintaining your home might seem like a financial drain each year, it's important to keep up with the maintenance so that it doesn't turn into a much bigger and more expensive deal. It's also important to maintain your home so that it continues to appreciate along with the rest of the neighborhood.

The maintenance of your home extends to your property lines, so don't forget your landscaping. My neighbor has an old, small house that's in dire need of repair. However, he has by far the most beautiful garden in the neighborhood. A few houses to the west, another neighbor sold her property in a bidding war within twenty-four hours, mostly because the condition of her house and landscaping was pristine. (She got several hundred thousand dollars more than any other house on the block has ever sold for.)

Your landscaping doesn't have to be fancy. But it does need to be pretty and green, well tended and healthy. If you live in the dry Southwest, choose plants that conserve water and fit in with the neighborhood landscape. If you live in a cold climate, make sure you keep your walks and driveway plowed in winter.

If you don't maintain your house and garden, your home essentially becomes a "fixer-upper." You won't profit as much from the sale of your home as you should, although the savvy buyer who takes your home off your hands and puts in the necessary work will reap the rewards.

A GOOD START

Walk around your home and take a long, hard look at its exterior. You are looking for cracks, holes, and chinks in the siding. Do you have moisture problems in the interior of your home? It's possible your windows may need caulking or sealing. Are you getting leaky drafts? You may need to caulk on the inside.

Are you having water problems when it rains? You might need to have your gutters cleaned out. Does water back up into your basement? You may need to root out your sewer line or you may need to regrade your landscaping so water flows away from the house. Look around the interior and exterior of your home for small maintenance issues that need to be taken care of to avoid turning a small problem into a big one. And remember, change your smoke detector and carbon monoxide batteries at least twice a year. Many people do this when the time changes from standard to daylight time and back again.

SIMPLE THING
33

SAVING FOR COLLEGE? CONSIDER PREPAID TUITION OR PREPAID SAVINGS PLANS

There are two truths when it comes to a college education these days: (1) getting a college degree is as necessary as getting a high school diploma a generation ago, and (2) it's going to be frightfully expensive no matter where your kid goes to school.

College tuition costs are rising between 5 to 7 percent per year. At this rate, they'll double in ten to fifteen years. So if an Ivy League education costs $35,000 per year today, you can expect a bill of at least $70,000 per year when your two-year-old is ready to go. State universities have always been a better deal, but even their costs are rising. Today the average cost of attending a public university (in-state tuition) is approximately $12,000. In fifteen years you could be paying $25,000 or more per year. Community colleges remain a bargain. The annual cost will be well under $10,000 per year fifteen years down the road. Which is fine if your child chooses a community college. (Heck, you can finally take that around-the-world trip!) But if you have your heart sent on sending your kids to Harvard, Stanford, or MIT (and who doesn't?), then you'd better figure out a way to put away enough to cover those kinds of tuitions and fees.

Obviously, one way is to save like crazy and invest those savings. But you should also consider prepaid tuition plans and college savings plans, also known as 529 plans.

Pay now, go later. That's what many state university prepaid tuition plans offer. You agree to prepay a certain amount of money today, in a lump sum or monthly installments, and Junior is guaranteed to have his ride paid for at one of the state schools.

Sounds great, but there are a couple of hitches. First, every state has its flagship university (the Urbana-Champaign campus of the University of Illinois, for example) and the rest of its state schools. Your child is guaranteed a place at *one* of the state schools, but not necessarily at his or her first choice.

Second, if your child decides not to go to school, you can pass the tuition "credits" or "units" to other children, or use them yourself. But if no one decides to go, or if all of your young geniuses get a free ride, then you get your cash back with about 2 percent interest. In other words, you'll get your principal back, but don't count this among your great investment experiences.

Finally, the growth of a prepaid tuition plan is essentially limited to how fast tuition, fees, and expenses are rising. Since the average cost for college increases 5 to 7 percent per year, if your cash today guarantees your child a place, that's how fast your money has to grow to keep pace. Historically, the stock market has returned about 11 percent per year. That's quite a bit of money to leave on the table over eighteen years.

State college savings plans can offer a higher return, and over the past five years, millions of parents have plunked billions of dollars into these plans. Many will allow your assets to grow to $100,000 or more, with federal taxes deferred and possibly no state taxes owed at all. The New York plan allows in-state participants to deduct as much as

$10,000 against state taxes (out-of-state residents don't qualify for this perk).

Another benefit is that these plans tend to invest for a much higher return. The fees are low (often below 1 percent), and typically the state hires a reputable investment manager. Some plans also allow you to choose between several mutual funds, each sporting a different amount of risk.

When you withdraw the cash, many programs allow you to pay tax at your child's rate rather than your own, which could be considerably less. In addition, you can transfer up to $50,000 per child in a single year free of gift tax if you're single, or up to $100,000 if you're married. (This is a proration of your $10,000 annual gift, tax-free). You can put in as little as $25 or $50 per month, or $250 per year.

How do these plans affect financial aid? All this could change over the years, but currently a prepaid tuition plan is treated as a pool of money to be used entirely to fund your child's college tuition—a dollar-for-dollar offset against financial aid. A college savings plan is treated as a parent's asset, of which the current financial aid formula requires you to spend 5.6 percent per year on your child's education.

What if you don't use the money? With a state college savings plan, funds not used for college are typically taxed at the parent's marginal tax rate and may be subject to a 10-to-15-percent penalty. With a prepaid tuition plan, your benefits may be reduced if your child attends an out-of-state university.

Overall, both of these plans are good choices, especially if they get you to save something to help your children with their education. By the time your grandchildren arrive, a college degree may no longer be sufficient to allow them to succeed in this world. The new minimum level of education might be a graduate degree.

A GOOD START

There are companies trying to figure out a way to tap into the huge need parents have for cash to pay college tuition bills. One program in the planning stage would have consumers sign up on its Web site, along with retailers and manufacturers of certain popular products, like Coca-Cola. The idea is that every time you purchase one of these items, a percentage of the value of the product would be deposited in a college savings account for your children.

Although none of these proposed programs was off the ground at press time, you should keep your eyes open for them. Think of them as resembling a credit card with a rebate program. If you use your card to purchase the item, your rebate comes back in the form of extra cash with which you can pay tuition.

DON'T BANKRUPT YOUR FUTURE TO PAY COLLEGE TUITION OR WEDDING BILLS

As parents, we have a deep instinct to help our children to survive and thrive. We want to help them become broad-minded adults, capable of living successful, happy lives. We want to share in their joys and sorrows and see them achieve everything we know they're capable of.

But when it comes to picking up the entire tab for college or for a wedding, consider these items as gifts, not obligations. If you'll never miss the cash, by all means go ahead and give your children these special gifts. If you're just scraping by, you may not be able to do so without breaking the bank.

Think about your retirement first. Buying a house could well set you on the right course, whereas diverting tens of thousands of dollars for tuition might keep you working for another decade. It's good to help, but don't do so at the expense of your financial well-being.

The truth is, your kids can borrow the cash they need for their college tuition. They can work part-time and go to school full-time, or they can work full-time and attend school at night. They can get financial aid, merit scholarships, and tuition waivers. When it comes time to get married, they can choose something less expensive—a homemade wedding, a simple ceremony, or eloping. They can even borrow cash to pay for a wedding.

But no one will ever lend you a dime for your retirement. And if you divert cash from your retirement savings to pay for college tuitions and weddings, you're the one who may suffer down the line.

A GOOD START

Determine how much you can afford to spend on your children's college tuition. Offer this assistance and then offer to help them find scholarships, loans, and even part-time jobs that will pay their way through school. While it would be nice to be able to afford to pay their complete tuition, you should know that plenty of students have loans and jobs to help carry this increasingly heavy load.

The worst thing you can do is to beat yourself up emotionally and psychologically. You may not be able to pay your children's total college tuition, but that doesn't mean you won't be there for them in a financially meaningful way at another point in their lives.

6

The Ins and Outs of Insurance

SIMPLE THING
35

BUY TERM INSURANCE
AND INVEST THE REST

Here's a piece of advice your insurance agent may not share with you: Not everyone needs life insurance. If you're single and no one depends on you financially for the daily necessities of life, you probably don't need life insurance. Or if you're fabulously wealthy, with loads of assets, you may not need it either.

If, on the other hand, you have a spouse, children, or perhaps dependent elderly parents, then you'll need to buy at least enough insurance to provide for their daily needs until they get to a point where they are independent and can survive alone.

Some employees get some life insurance through work. Usually it equals a year or two of your annual salary. If you earn $60,000 per year, you might get a life insurance policy worth $60,000 to $120,000. That might sound like a lot, but if you have two kids and a stay-at-home spouse, it won't last long—even if your spouse also gets your monthly (or lump sum) pension and social security.

Tally up what you spend on all the big items in a given year, like mortgage, car payments, tuition, utilities, child care, or other outstanding loans. Does the number surprise you? Now add up which of these expenses will disappear if you suddenly pass away. Which other long-term or short-term expenses will be added in?

If your family's annual expenses will continue to be $60,000 after you're gone, and you want your family to continue living in the lifestyle to which they've become accustomed (or better), you'll need to buy enough insurance to replace your income each year, adjusted for inflation. This is the cash your family will depend on after you're gone.

Two Insurance Options

There are two basic types of life insurance policies: term insurance and whole-life insurance.

Term insurance is a one-year policy you can purchase relatively inexpensively. If you're a healthy nonsmoker, aged thirty-five to forty, $500,000 worth of life insurance might cost you less than $500 per year. If you die within the year, the policy pays off. If you don't die, then you live to pay your premium for the following year.

Whole-life insurance comes in a variety of flavors, including whole-life, variable whole-life, and universal whole-life. They all boil down to the same two components: insurance and savings. The savings component is invested in a mutual fund. With variable whole-life and universal whole-life, you essentially have a wider choice of mutual funds.

Regardless of the variety, whole-life insurance is extremely expensive. The commission is often equal to one and a half times the cost of the first year's premium, and there are renewal commissions as well. Also, you pay a stiff management fee to the mutual fund for the savings component.

The bottom line is, if you don't keep your whole-life policy for at least twenty to twenty-five years, it's not worth the money. And when you're young and you most need the coverage, it's difficult to be able to afford enough whole-life insurance to protect your family. I'm not a big fan of whole-life insurance.

In contrast, term insurance is cheap. You can buy it with a fixed price (called a "level load") over a long period of time, say ten to thirty years. Once you buy the insurance, the price never changes, even if you get sick.

So figure out how much it really costs you to live, and purchase enough term insurance to give your loved ones enough cash to continue to live at least as well as they are doing now, or perhaps a bit better. Take whatever else you would have spent on a whole-life policy and invest it yourself in a solidly rated mutual fund (go to Morningstar.net for mutual fund information). You'll wind up with a whole lot more coverage, for a whole lot less money.

A GOOD START

Go online to one of the big insurance sites, such as Insweb.com, Quotesmith.com, or MasterQuote.com, and apply for term life insurance. Filling out the form should take you all of fifteen to twenty minutes. The company will contact you to set up your medical exam.

It's easy to start the process of looking for insurance and then get derailed when you start playing mental games about what life will be like after you die. It may not be fun shopping for life insurance, but you'll hardly ever make a more important decision.

RAISE YOUR DEDUCTIBLES

The problem with auto or homeowner's insurance is that if you use it—that is, if you actually have a claim—you may either be dropped by the company or your policy cost might skyrocket. The smart way to think about insurance is as a safety net that helps you out in a catastrophe, rather than as a way to resolve small problems and issues.

Since you'll be paying for most small problems out of your own pocket, you should raise the deductible (the out-of-pocket) expense on your auto and homeowner's insurance policies. That will have the side benefit of lowering your annual premiums.

How high should the deductible be? Start by looking at how much the policy will cost at each deductible level. For example, with a $250 deductible your auto insurance might cost $600 every six months, or $1,200 per year. If you raise the deductible to $500, your annual insurance policy might drop to $1,000 per year, or $500 every six months. By raising your deductible $250, you've lowered the cost of your insurance premium by $200.

The same thing happens with your homeowner's insurance policy. You might pay $1,200 per year with a $250 deductible, or $1,000 per year with a $500 deductible. If you take the extra $200 saved each year, and put it into a separate account, you'll be able to fund some of the minor things that need to be fixed in a house each year. When your sump pump fails and your basement floods, you'll be responsible for the first $500 of expenses, but the insurance will cover the rest.

When you talk to your insurance agent (or go online), play around with the numbers and see where you're most comfortable. Look back over your auto and home-repair expenses over the past few years and see how much they've really cost you. Then you'll be able to make a financially savvy choice.

A GOOD START

Call your insurance company and ask how much your premium would be if you raised the deductible. Remember, you'll need to cover the cost of the deductible yourself, so make it a number that you're comfortable with. For example, if you raise your deductible from $250 to $500, you'll be responsible for the first $500 worth of damage. While you may be able to scrape up $500, it may be a lot tougher for you to come up with $1,000.

CONSOLIDATE INSURANCE COMPANIES AND SAVE

There are several ways to pay less for the insurance premiums you need:

1. **Shop around for the best deal.** It's possible to buy homeowner's and automobile insurance online from a number of reputable sources. Use your computer to shop the Internet for the best deals and compare quotes.

2. **Raise your deductible.** As we just discussed, if you raise your deductible from, say, $250 to $500 or $1,000, you can lower your annual premium substantially. Remember, you're responsible for paying up to the deductible, so make sure it's a number with which you're comfortable.

3. **Install a home security system.** Many insurers will lower your premium by 5 percent if you install a home security system. When shopping around for policies, ask the insurer what you would have to do to qualify for this discount.

4. **Get a senior's discount (if you're over fifty-five).** Many insurance companies perceive seniors as being less of a risk when it comes to homeowner's

and automobile insurance. Ask the agent how old you have to be to qualify.

5. **Take special classes offered by many insurance companies.** Insurance companies will often offer home safety or automobile safety classes. If you take one of these courses, you may receive a discount of up to 5 percent on your premium.

6. **Insure your home, not the land it's on.** The concept here is that even if your house is completely destroyed, the land value will remain intact. (It's not as if some alien is going to cut your lot out of the earth and cart it away somewhere.) So if you paid $200,000 for your home, some of that is the value of the home, and the rest is the value of the lot. You'll need to determine exactly how much your home is worth and (more to the point) how much it will cost to rebuild it to today's standards. If you have a 2,000-square-foot house on the lot, to rebuild that house might cost $100 per square foot, or $200,000—the full price you paid. On the other hand, if you have a 2,000-square-foot house on a lot that is now worth $500,000 because of its location, it would still cost $200,000 to rebuild your home. Ask your insurance agent for guidance. Or you can call a local builder to get more information on building costs in the area.

7. **Stop smoking.** Almost all insurance companies give discounts to homeowners who don't smoke, because the risk of a fire starting from a cigarette ember is so high. In addition to the benefit of saving you $1,460 per year for each pack-a-day you give up, you may also receive a discount on your medical insurance.

A GOOD START

There are two other things you can do to lower your insurance premium cost: consolidate insurers and become a good customer.

Insurance companies have tremendous costs of doing business. They have to find customers, get those customers to buy policies, pay out claims and expenses, and find a way to keep customers. If you buy all of your insurance policies (or most of them) from the same insurance company, it's a cheaper way for them to do business. And many companies are happy to share that cost savings with you by lowering the cost of your insurance policy.

How much can you save? If you buy your homeowner's, auto, general liability, and business liability (if you have a home office, for example) from the same company, you may be able to save as much as 5 to 15 percent on your premium costs. But beware—some states don't allow discounts on premiums. (That's all about politics and money.)

The other way to save money is to stick around. If you've kept your coverage with the same insurer for years, you should ask your agent, or company representative, if they have a discount for longevity. Some insurance companies will give discounts of up to 5 or 6 percent if you've been a policyholder for six years or more.

If you don't ask, you'll never know.

7

Taxing Taxes

SIMPLE THING

38

DO YOUR OWN TAXES
AT LEAST ONCE

The worst thing about doing your taxes isn't actually doing them. It's the long, slow buildup *before* you do them, starting on or about April 16 of the previous year. It's during that time when fear sets in and your insecurities pop out.

Knowing that you have to find all of your records, receipts, bank statements, mutual-fund statements, and scraps of paper on which you wrote the purchase and sales prices of stock is, well, a little scary. What if you can't find everything? What if you don't add it all up right?

This year it's going to be different. If you've been following the Simple Things suggestions in this book, you've already organized all of your record-keeping. You've created files for your bills, receipts, and bank and mutual-fund statements. Perhaps you've even started using software to track your expenses.

When the time comes to gather this information for this year's taxes, you've already done all of the hard work. It'll be easy for you to go to your mutual-fund statement file and pull out what you need. You'll go to your computer and instantly know how much you've spent this year. If you chose Quicken as your financial software, you might even be able to upload your information right into their TurboTax software, which should make doing your taxes a snap.

But even if you haven't gotten that far (remember, working on your personal finances should be an evolution, not a revolution), you'll be well positioned to pull together your paperwork and tackle your own taxes.

Why should you? Doing your own taxes gives you an inside look at exactly what you're paying Uncle Sam each year. You'll learn how tax brackets work, what deductions and credits may be available to you, and how the numbers get calculated.

But the biggest benefit in doing your own taxes is that you don't have to pay someone else to do them for you. And that's money you can save year in and year out.

A GOOD START

If you chose Quicken as your money-management software, purchase a copy of TurboTax. Install the program. It will lead you through a series of questions about your finances, home, dependents, write-offs, and other items. At the end it will compute your taxes owed all on its own. There is a help line you can call as well.

If you've tried to do your taxes yourself, and the result either seems wrong or you can't get through it, you'll still have your regular taxpaying option—and you'll only be out the cost of the software. Whatever option you choose, don't procrastinate. You want to leave enough time to start over if you've made a mistake or call for help if you need it. You don't want to get hit with late-filing fees.

DON'T GIVE UNCLE SAM AN INTEREST-FREE LOAN

If you count on receiving a big refund from Uncle Sam each year, you should give yourself forty lashes with a wet noodle. That's because you've just given Uncle Sam an interest-free loan. The way you do this is by overpaying on your taxes throughout the year.

The problem with overpaying on your taxes is that the federal government is enjoying the free use of your money. If you'd actually paid only what you really owed, the extra cash might have been sitting around in your account, earning interest for you. (It's that principal again of making your money work harder—so you don't have to.)

Over the years, many folks have told me they like getting that check back from the IRS and have even come to depend on it to pay off the last of the holiday shopping bills or to pay for a spring-break trip with their kids.

But that's the wrong way to think about your money. If you're charging more than you can repay at the end of a month, you need to readjust your spending habits, not depend on a check back from the government.

How can you adjust what you pay the government? If you're an employee, you have a portion of your income withheld from each paycheck. This amount is based on the number of "withholding allowances" you selected when you first went to work at this company. You're entitled to take a standard deduction for yourself and your spouse (if you have one), and a deduction for each of your children. The idea is that if you have a family of four (you, your spouse, and two kids), then the withholding from your check will have automatically taken the amount of these deductions into account, and you'll end up just about even at tax time.

But sometimes this number doesn't work out just right. If, for example, you itemize your deductions, you may end up paying less in tax than would be expected from someone who simply takes the standard deductions. In this case you might get a check back from Uncle Sam about six weeks after you file your income tax statement.

Since the idea is to end up even (or have to write a small check to the IRS at tax time), you'll want to adjust your withholdings. Talk to your human resources department about what paperwork you need to fill out in order to correct your IRS imbalance.

If you're self-employed, you'll need to file and pay quarterly estimates of the annual tax you'll owe. If you've overpaid during the year, it's not as bad simply because you may elect to transfer the overpayment to your first quarterly estimate, which is also due on April 15, the same day your tax return is due.

Once again, don't look at your overpayment of taxes as enforced savings, or a government-sponsored "pay off your Christmas bills in April" campaign. All you've done is give the government an interest-free loan, which might be in their best financial interest—but isn't in yours.

A GOOD START

If you work for a company, see the person in human resources who oversees your paycheck and deductions. Make sure you adjust the withholdings so that you're withholding just enough from your paycheck, given any deductions or credits you may have, and the size of your family, to cover the taxes you'll owe next April.

FIGHT YOUR PROPERTY
TAXES EACH YEAR

If you own a home, you pay property taxes based on a portion of its true value. (This varies from state to state.) Unless you live in California, where your property taxes are permanently pegged to the amount you paid for your home (with a few exceptions for major renovations and additions), or another state where there are similar caps on property taxes, you'll watch your property tax bill rise each year.

While property taxes are expensive, they're not optional. If you fail to pay your property taxes, you could very well lose your house. What you need to do is focus on getting your property taxes lowered so that you're not paying more than your fair share.

Although the procedure differs slightly from state to state, the concept of how to fight your property taxes remains the same. When you receive your notice of taxes owed for the coming year, you'll generally have about thirty days to file an appeal.

You can usually appeal your taxes on one of several grounds: if there are errors in the property report (for example, if the report lists your house as having five bedrooms when you have three, or four full baths when you only have three); if other homes in the neighborhood that fall into your home's tax classification are paying less than you are; or if your home isn't worth what the tax assessor thinks it's worth.

Each state has its own procedure for fighting property taxes, and you should check with your local tax assessor for information and pamphlets that explain what steps you need to take, how you need to document your claim, and when you need to file your appeal.

If you aren't satisfied with the tax relief the assessor's office gives you, you may continue to file appeals several more times. In some states you'll wind up at the state supreme court. In others you'll wind up at the state board of appeals.

The best part about trying to get your tax bill lowered is that there are cumulative effects. Not only do you pay less in the year that your appeal is granted, but in subsequent years you'll pay less because the base tax was lowered. For the amount of work you'll do (and there is some work to be done), you may save yourself thousands of dollars in property taxes.

You should be aware that there are some folks (typically real-estate attorneys) who will offer to fight your property taxes in exchange for a third or a half of whatever you save in the first year. So if you get your property taxes lowered by $1,000, you'd owe the attorney $333 or $500, as per your agreement. (Of course, the county may or may not send you a check for the difference, meaning you may have to pay the attorney out of your own pocket.) The truth is, it isn't that difficult to appeal your property taxes. Try doing it yourself the first time. You may be surprised by how easy the whole process is.

A GOOD START

Newspapers usually publish an area's tax rolls when the new tax bills are announced. You'll want to look in your local paper, which will give you the address and tax number of each property, plus its property category and the amount of the tax bill.

From there, it's up to you to make your case in front of the tax assessor. You'll need to take photographs of other homes in the same property tax category as yours, and that are about the same size and in the same condition as yours, but are paying less in taxes than you are.

Your next step is to assemble a little photograph display that shows exactly why your home is being overtaxed compared to properties that are similar.

It's important to protest your taxes at the right time. Usually, you'll have thirty to sixty days to protest your tax bill (you'll still have to pay the current bill—if you get a reduction, it will come off future bills). If you miss the deadline for protesting, you'll have to wait until the following year.

— 8 —

Marriage, Partnership, and Children

SIMPLE THING
41

SHARE YOUR FAMILY'S MONEY MANAGEMENT DUTIES

Do you know what's going on with your family's finances? Take this quick quiz to find out:

1. What is your annual family income?
2. How much money do you save each year (including retirement accounts and other savings)?
3. How much do you spend on groceries each week?
4. How much money do you spend on vacations each year?
5. Do you know where the key to your safe deposit box is? And can you name the entire contents of your safe deposit box?
6. Do you know the named beneficiaries on your spouse's life insurance policy and retirement accounts?
7. What percentage of your income did you pay in taxes last year?
8. What is the single most expensive item you or a member of your family bought last year?
9. Do you know what your family's net worth is?
10. What is your spouse's social security number?

If you can't answer at least nine of these ten questions with reasonable accuracy, you're probably not involved enough in your family's finances.

Paying Bills and a Whole Lot More

Do you hold the family checkbook? Or does your spouse or partner take care of paying your monthly bills. Do you jointly make decisions about insurance, saving money, and investments? Or have these jobs been assigned, over time, to you or your better half?

For some people, paying the bills each month (and having the money to do so) is a joy, not a job. For others, unopened bills pile up in a shoebox until a red envelope arrives, threatening to shut off your electricity. (By the way, if this is you, get an automatic bill-paying service, or put all of your utility bills on a credit card so you only have one or two checks to write each month.)

Even if one spouse or partner writes the checks, it's a good idea for both of you to be completely involved with your family's finances. You should both know what you have, where you have it, what interest rate you're paying on your loans, and what rate of return you're receiving on your investments. You should have written and signed a will (particularly if children are involved), and you should spend at least one evening every six months assessing where you are on the way toward achieving your financial goals.

Ask yourself these questions: Are you on track to achieving your goals? If not, is there some tweaking with the family budget or your investments that can help get you where you want to go?

Throughout the years, I've had dozens and dozens of letters from widows (it's usually women) who have been left bereft emotionally and financially. They had left the money-management decisions to their husband, and one day, after their spouse is gone, they woke up to discover they had no idea what they had to live on.

No matter how much money you have, both you and your partner need to take an active role in managing it.

A GOOD START

There are better times and worse times to have a talk about your own personal finances. Don't talk about your money under any of these conditions:

1. When there are distractions. These include Sunday football (or another sport), when small children are underfoot, if you're entertaining friends or family, or if your parents or in-laws are visiting.

2. If you or your spouse or partner is in a bad mood, angry, or frustrated over a work issue; or if one of you is sick, or is traveling for business (unless something really urgent comes up).

3. When you or your spouse or partner is overemotional or not able to discuss the numbers rationally, for whatever reason.

The best time to talk about money, of course, is before you make a life commitment to each other: when you're feeling good, in a comfortable place, and have your whole life ahead of you. If you're a bit beyond that, choose a time when the kids are asleep, or if the two of you can steal away for a few hours. Once you start talking about money, you should plan on regular discussions (perhaps weekly, perhaps every other week), to keep the momentum going.

The toughest time to talk about money is when you don't have any. In this case, try not to be angry if you are in your current financial position because of something your spouse or partner did. Accusations and a lot of yelling won't make for a productive conversation.

HIRE YOUR SPOUSE
OR CHILDREN

Enterprising individuals will often start small, home-based businesses. Such businesses may develop out of a hobby or a low-cost idea. My friend Rick loves to do wood-working. He joined up with an artist friend of his to create hand-painted kids' furniture. He also helps small companies update their Web sites.

If you have a business, you're allowed to deduct the expenses of running the business before you pay tax on your profits. That includes the cost of paying employees or independent contractors.

On the flip side, each individual who earns less than $95,000 per year (less than $160,000 if you're married) has the ability to open up a Roth IRA account. You can put away up to $2,000 per year (up to $4,000 if you're married) in after-tax earned income, which will then grow tax-free for life. (See Simple Thing 47.)

If you hire your children (or your spouse, for that matter) to do a real job for your home-based business, the IRS will permit you to pay them for their work. If you then open up an IRA in your child's name, you can put away up to $2,000 of the income they earned from your business. It's a win-win situation for everyone. You get some much-needed help with your home-based business, you're spending quality time with your child, and you save on taxes.

Your children get to put away money that will help them much later in life, and they feel as though they're really contributing to the family.

As the saying goes, youth is a wonderful thing. If, starting at age ten, your child puts away just $1,200 per year, and that money grows at just 10 percent per year, by the time he or she is sixty, that'll add up to nearly $1.4 million. (And your child will have contributed just $60,000 over the course of those fifty years.) That's the power of compounding capital. If your offspring puts away just $2,000 in a single year, and the money grows untouched at 10 percent for thirty years, he or she will have in excess of $35,000. Even with inflation, that will be enough money to buy something substantial.

A GOOD START

As this book was going to press, legislation was before Congress that would raise the Roth IRA and conventional IRA limits to $5,000 each, or $10,000 per couple. This legislation hadn't passed at press time, but be on the lookout for these numbers to go up. Putting away an extra $3,000 per person per year could mean you'd earn tens (or even hundreds) of thousands of extra dollars over the life of the account.

If you work for someone else, it may be difficult to hire your children. But you can still give them the gift of a Roth IRA—if they hold a part-time job. If your daughter or son delivers newspapers, for example, you can make a Roth IRA contribution for him or her (as long as your family income falls under the phase-out threshold) up to the amount earned (or $2,000, whichever is lower). So if they earn $1,500 one summer, you can deposit $1,500 into a Roth IRA for them.

TALK ABOUT MONEY WITH YOUR SPOUSE, KIDS, AND PARENTS

In our society, there are still strict taboos about money. We'll talk about sex, drugs, and politics, but when it comes to money, many folks button their lips. Which would be all right if you were talking to strangers or even your neighbors over the backyard fence. The trouble is, many folks don't even talk to their spouses or partners about money. And that's the root of many money troubles in relationships.

There once was a businessman who found himself in a huge mess. He had been quite successful and managed the entire family's finances. He gave his wife loads of expensive presents and a charge card with a very high limit. Over the years, she furnished their house distinctively, dressed herself, him, and their children beautifully, entertained lavishly, and booked expensive vacations.

The only problem was that, somewhere along the way, this man's business started to fail. Instead of talking about it with his wife, he pretended that he was still bringing in the big bucks. Completely unaware of the change in their financial circumstances, she kept charging like crazy. Until the moment of truth: Sitting in their accountant's office, he broke the news to his wife that not only were they in tremendous debt, but they were likely to have to declare bankruptcy. Stunned, his wife sat there. Then she burst into tears as he told her how his fortunes had changed.

"Why didn't you tell me?" she cried.

The man sat there for a while and finally said, "I didn't want you to think I was a failure."

The funny thing is, if the wife and husband had shared equally in the management of their money, this couple might not have lost everything. When things started to slow down in his businesses, she would have known to keep a lid on their spending. Together they could have decided to sell their large house and move to someplace more affordable. They could have sold some artwork, or she could have gone back to work to help get the family back on its feet.

Do you talk to your spouse or partner about money? Did you feel funny asking how much the other earned while you were dating? Do you feel funny asking about it now? Here are some questions every spouse or partner should ask of their loved one:

1. How much do you earn each year?
2. How much do you have saved in retirement accounts?
3. How much do you have saved outside of your retirement accounts?
4. How much debt do you have?
5. How much life insurance do you have (or does your job provide any)?

These are just the basic questions to ask. But it's also important to know what kind of gifts your spouse or partner likes to give or receive, how much risk he or she likes to take with investments, and what his or her financial goals and expectations are.

When she was single, Melissa worked on Wall Street. When she married a successful trader, he gave her the option of staying home when they had children. But he asked her to manage their family's finances. With her Wall Street background, he assumed she'd be a risk-taker with their finances, especially with money they wouldn't need for twenty years or more. Five years and two kids later, he discovered that all of the bills were being paid on time, but that she'd invested all of their money in certificates of deposit (CDs) and zero-coupon bonds. He had expected most of their long-term investments would be in the stock market.

So don't assume that because you know what kind of gift your spouse or partner likes to get that you know his or her innermost feelings about money. You have to ask.

Kids and Money

Hard as it is to talk to your kids about sex, most parents never even broach the subject of money with their children. And that's a crucial mistake. Children should be slowly introduced to the concept of money and money management well before they're ten. As they get older and assume more responsibility, their parents should share with them some of the information surrounding the family's financial affairs.

How much information is too much? Your teenagers probably don't need to know exactly what your mortgage payment is, but they should know what a mortgage is, and that you have one on your property. They should understand that a portion of what they earn at their summer or part-time job is paid in taxes, and that they should start putting money away for college tuition and retirement as soon as possible. In their twenties and thirties you'll want them to know what you have, how you've decided to divvy it up (especially if you're not leaving everything equally to your children, or if there are other heirs), where the important documents are, and how the kids can get hold of them in case of emergency. You may even wish to add your children as signatories to your lock box at the bank. They should also know that you simply cannot afford to buy them everything they want.

If you don't talk to your children about money, you'll never know how they feel about it. And they won't know how you've struggled for it and why you value it as much as you do.

Parents and Money

If it's almost impossible to talk to your children about money, it's even more difficult for some adults to talk to their aging parents about their money. But as today's baby boomers turn into the sandwich generation (caring for adult children and aging parents at the same time), it's more important than ever for them to break through the money taboo and talk to their parents about their finances.

It's especially important if you're caring for elderly parents who have a physical or mental disability such as Alzheimer's disease. You may need to gain a power of attorney over their estate in order to liquidate assets to pay nursing home or medical bills. You may need to help them budget so that their money lasts as long as it needs to. If they don't have enough to cover a long-term-care facility, you may wish to purchase long-term-care insurance for them, in order to assure yourself (and them) that you won't go bankrupt picking up a much larger bill.

Start talking to your parents about what they have and where they have it. Find out who their accountant and attorneys are. Make sure you have a complete list of assets and accounts, and update this list every six months to a year (depending on the age and health of your parents). Make sure they've signed their wills (and living wills), or have put their assets into a living trust. Finally, make sure your parents know you're doing this for them—not for yourself.

A GOOD START

If you think it's tough to talk to your spouse or partner about money, try broaching the subject with your parents. Unfortunately, some parents are less receptive to having this conversation than others. Those parents who are of the "old school," where money was inherited but not talked about, will probably be the least receptive.

Still, you have to have the conversation. If they refuse, talk to their lawyer and doctor about stressing the importance of updating wills and a list of assets, creating powers of attorney for their health care and finances, and structuring their estate so that the burden of distributing the assets and closing the estate is as easy as possible in a difficult situation.

GIVE SIGNIFICANT GIFTS

When my parents were first married, my great-aunt Ruth asked my father what he intended to give my mother for an anniversary present. When he replied that he didn't know, she gave him this piece of advice: Give significant gifts.

Aunt Ruth's point is savvy from a financial point of view. Significant gifts are remembered and treasured. And, they needn't be expensive (though many are). The key here is to make the gift a sentimental keepsake.

For our first anniversary I gave my husband, Sam, a silver money clip from Tiffany's. I was in the first year of my writing business and wasn't making much money. But I wanted to give him something he'd use, something significant. I had the money clip engraved with his initials on one side and the date of our anniversary on the other. I also wanted to engrave it with my name, but each letter was another ten dollars. I didn't have enough money, so I had it engraved "love, I." Thirteen years later he still treasures that gift above any other I've given him.

The idea here is not to plunk down the big bucks for a present that screams "expensive," or to keep laying out for a steady stream of forgettable gifts. It's to save money by giving fewer but more significant gifts whose impact outweighs the cost.

Significant gifts don't have to be jewelry. You could set aside the cash and use it as a down payment on a home. It could be a special vacation you've been planning for, or it could be renovating your bathroom. It could be a memory box of photos and trinkets that you've decorated with cut-up photos of your friends and family, or the conversion of family slides to video.

For each person, the word "significant" has a different meaning. When I was pregnant with our son, Alex, it was a terribly hot, humid summer. For my birthday, Sam gave me two huge new air conditioners for our old house. I used them nonstop for three months. It may be the most important gift he's ever given me. (And today, now that we have central air, we often talk about those window units and laugh.)

There's always a time and place to give that special someone small, frivolous gifts. But when it comes to gift-giving, on your anniversary or during the holidays, it's better to give a significant gift, or pool your money to buy a significant joint gift.

Over time, the pleasure at receiving a small gift fades away. (Can you remember every gift your spouse or partner has ever given you?) But a significant gift is treasured forever.

A GOOD START

It's important to find out what kinds of gifts your spouse or partner expects to receive, and what kinds of gifts he or she likes to give in return. While it's nice to be surprised, as the years go on, it's also nice to coordinate gifts and perhaps buy something meaningful together, or give yourselves a memorable vacation.

It's also important to find ways to give gifts that are inexpensive but thoughtful—particularly if you shower all of your children, nieces, and nephews with gifts at the holidays. What this requires mostly is creativity and forethought. For example, all children love objects that have their names on them. It may be most economical to buy a dozen plastic mugs, plates, bowls, or other objects, and have someone decorate them with the children's names.

Creativity isn't expensive. But you have to spend the time to create something significant that won't empty your pocketbook.

WRITE AND SIGN
YOUR WILL

A will is a legal document that determines how your assets (cash, furniture, jewelry, stocks, house, car, etc.) will be distributed after your death. You don't need a will for assets that have a named beneficiary (like life insurance or a retirement account), assets that are in a trust, or assets that are jointly owned with rights of survivorship, since these will pass directly to the co-owner. (This doesn't take those assets out of your estate for tax purposes; it just means your will doesn't control what happens to them and they will bypass probate.)

If you don't have all of your assets in a trust, or if you don't have named beneficiaries, your will becomes extremely important. If you have minor children, you can name guardians for them in your will. Without this, the court will determine who gets custody of your children (and control of the funds you've left them in your will).

If you die intestate (without a will), the court will determine who gets what, based on the state formula. In many states your spouse will get half of your estate, and your children will divide the other half. If you have no children, your spouse will get half and your parents may get half, and so on.

When you write a will, you are affirming, in a legal way, what you want to happen after your death. This is an extremely difficult thing to do, and many people are reluctant to tackle these "life after death" issues. But if you have considerable assets, or if you have minor children, you will want to make sure your wishes are followed. A will is the only way in which to do this legally.

A GOOD START

You can get a preprinted will from your local stationery store, but you must make sure it is one that is valid for your state. (Each state has its own requirements.) Another option is to hire an estate attorney to write a will for you that will be legally binding.

Typically, you'll need at least two or three individuals to witness your signing of the will. These individuals should not be beneficiaries of the will, or a court could rule it invalid. Keep one original of your will in your safe deposit box, and another with your attorney. You may also need to find a notary to execute the will.

Once you have a will, especially if you have young children, you'll find that a huge burden has been lifted off you. You'll know that your wishes will be followed. But don't make this mistake: Having a will doesn't mean that you've minimized estate taxes. All it means is that your heirs will receive the assets you've left them, minus court costs and probate fees.

If you want to minimize estate taxes, you first need to know how much you have. If your net worth exceeds $700,000 (this number will rise to $1 million by 2006 according to current law, but this could change, so keep your eyes open), including life insurance proceeds, you may wish to talk to an estate planner to find out how you can minimize estate taxes.

Each individual is allowed to pass down a certain amount of assets tax-free. By 2006, it will be $1 million each. (It is possible that at some point, estate taxes will be wiped out for all but the super-rich, or perhaps for everyone). Current tax law permits a spouse to inherit any amount, tax-free. (This is not yet available to life partners.) If you leave everything to your spouse, however, he or she can still only pass down $1 million (in 2006) tax-free, and so you've lost an opportunity to pass down a total of $2 million tax-free (your $1 million and your spouse's $1 million).

With the right kind of estate planning, you can create a trust that will pay your spouse the income on your $1 million for his or her lifetime, but actually leave the funds to your children or another heir. Talk to an estate attorney for more details.

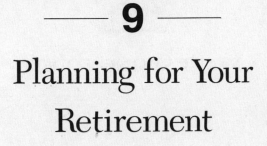

9

Planning for Your Retirement

START SAVING TODAY

I recently told my son, Alex, the story of the tortoise and the hare for the first time. I explained that the moral of the story is to pace yourself—slow and steady wins the race.

The same is true when it comes to your financial life. If you start putting money away for your retirement when you're in your twenties (or even in your teens), you can put away smaller sums throughout the years, but end up with far more.

The numbers tell the story. Assume a 10-percent average annual return. Your actual return may differ slightly due to monthly compounding, or if you achieve a higher return earlier on in the process (like five years of 20-percent-plus returns in the 1990s).

Years	$100/ Month	$200/ Month	$300/ Month	$400/ Month	$500/ Month
10	$ 19,125	$ 38,250	$ 57,375	$ 76,500	$ 95,625
20	68,730	137,460	206,190	274,920	343,650
30	197,393	394,786	592,179	789,572	986,965
40	531,111	1,062,222	1,593,333	2,124,444	2,655,555
50	1,396,690	2,793,380	4,190,070	5,586,760	6,983,450

The results are stunning. And for those of you who don't imagine you'll have fifty years of compounding ahead of you, if you start putting away $100 per month (only $1,200 per year) when you're twenty-five, you'll be only seventy-five when your investment of $60,000 (fifty years × $1,200 per year) is worth nearly $1.4 million. Putting away $500 per month (or $6,000 per year) will allow you to harvest nearly $7 million on your investment of just $300,000.

You'll be very wealthy—and that doesn't even include the value of your home (which, by that time, will probably be all paid off).

Okay, here's the downside: Inflation will eat away a portion of that return. Still, you're far better off having it than not. And even in fifty years, $7 million will still be a sizable chunk of change in addition to other retirement funds, savings or inheritances you may have, or pension or social security you may also receive.

Does it seem unlikely that at age twenty-five you might be able to salt away $100 or $250 per month? Perhaps, but the earlier you are when you start saving for your retirement, the easier it is to let the magic of compounding work throughout your lifetime.

The later you start saving for retirement, the harder it is to come up with the same kind of dollars. You'll have to put away many multiples of these relatively reasonable figures to achieve the same sorts of results. That's because the magic of compounding—letting your money sit there and earn interest on itself over the years—works in your favor.

A GOOD START

I'm often asked when is the best time to start saving for retirement. The answer, of course, is today. If you wait ten years, five years, or even until next year to start putting money away, you'll have to save that much more to achieve your financial goals.

But if you invest steadily throughout the years, and earn a reasonable 10-percent return, you'll end up wealthier than you ever imagined.

Start today. If you can, put away the maximum allowed into your 401(k) or other retirement pension plan at work. If you don't have a 401(k) or pension plan option available to you, open up an IRA or a Roth IRA (see Simple Thing 47).

Any financial institution will allow you to open up a retirement account. And it will have all sorts of information that explains the options available to you.

If possible, have the cash withdrawn electronically every month from your checking account or, better yet, taken directly from your paycheck. It will be that much easier to save and invest your money.

SIMPLE THING

47

OPEN UP A ROTH IRA

Think of the Roth IRA as a new take on the old IRA for a new generation of future retirees. You can contribute up to $2,000 (plus another $2,000 for your spouse) of after-tax money. (As we went to press, there was talk about raising this limit to $5,000 for each individual, and perhaps indexing for inflation.)

The initial contribution isn't tax-deductible, but grows tax-free as long as you meet these withdrawal requirements: You must be age fifty-nine or older, and the account must have been open at least five years.

You may withdraw your contributions tax-free and penalty-free if you're fifty-nine or older. However, if you are under age fifty-nine and you withdraw some of the earnings, you may owe tax on the earnings plus a 10-percent penalty.

As with any rules, there are some exceptions: First-time home buyers may withdraw up to $10,000 penalty-free to use for a down payment or to pay closing costs. You can also withdraw funds to pay college or graduate school tuition for yourself, your spouse, or your children or grand-children, or if you are paying medical expenses that exceed 7.5 percent of your adjusted gross income.

High-income individuals (whose income exceeds $110,000 for a single person or $160,000 for married cou-ples filing jointly) aren't eligible to open a Roth IRA. And the benefit of a Roth IRA starts declining when your individual income exceeds $95,000 and your joint income exceeds $150,000.

One of the best things about a Roth IRA is that you never have to withdraw from the account. With a conventional IRA, you must begin withdrawals when you reach the age of 70½, and if you don't withdraw the minimum annual amount, you could be hit with a penalty that is 50 percent of the amount you should have withdrawn. If you don't need the money, a Roth IRA gets you around those mandatory withdrawals. In addition, you can continue to contribute to a Roth IRA as long as you have earned income.

Roth IRAs can also be a great estate-planning tool. Unlike a conventional IRA, if your Roth IRA has cash in it when you die, the account passes to your heirs income tax-free, no matter how much you have in the account. However, it will be considered as part of your estate, which may be subject to estate taxes.

A GOOD START

Opening a Roth IRA isn't very difficult. You simply choose a financial institution (preferably one that has a multitude of investment options, like Fidelity, Charles Schwab, or Vanguard) and set up an account.

Take your initial contribution to the financial institution of your choice. How much do you need initially? Some institutions require $1,000 to open up a Roth IRA, but others will do it for less, and others require just a fifty-dollar minimum deposit, as long as you allow the institution to make regular electronic withdrawals from your account.

What some people don't understand is that once you open the Roth IRA, your funds are sitting in what is essentially a money-market account. They're in cash, waiting for you to invest them in something. So choose a mutual fund (check Morningstar.com for a load of information on mutual funds) that gets high ratings, has at least a fifteen-year track record for performing well, so you can sleep at night, and put your Roth IRA cash into that mutual fund.

You can direct the financial institution to invest the money it withdraws electronically from your account directly into the mutual fund each month. That way, you don't have to make a separate call to direct the investment yourself.

One of the best things you can do is to open a Roth IRA for your children just as soon as they start earning income from babysitting or newspaper delivery jobs. Because of the exponential benefits of saving from the earliest age possible, you could be giving them a multi-million-dollar gift for their retirement years, long after you're gone.

SIMPLE THING
48

TAKE FULL ADVANTAGE OF ANY
EMPLOYER-MATCHING PROGRAMS

One of the easiest things you can do to maximize your retirement dollars is to fund your 401(k) or 403(b) (if you
work for a nonprofit organization or the government) retirement fund to the hilt. That's because your contribution is deducted from your paycheck before it ever reaches
you. The cash is electronically dumped into your retirement account, where it grows, and grows, and grows.

If your employer offers to match your contributions up
to a certain amount, this terrific deal becomes even better.
That's because an employer match (whether in cash or in
company stock) is like getting free money. If your employer will match you fifty cents on the dollar up to the
first $3,000 in contributions, that's an additional $1,500
you wouldn't otherwise have had. You're starting off the
year with a 50-percent return on your money *in addition to*
the return you'll earn on top of that.

So take full advantage of your employer's matching program. It could be the easiest money you'll earn all year.

I'm often asked whether it pays to invest in your 401(k) if
your employer doesn't match your contributions at all. The
answer is yes. It's always better to put away as many pre-tax
dollars as you can, and have them grow tax-free over many
years. The more cash you have, the faster it grows.

Although you will likely have to pay some tax on this cash when you draw the money in retirement, you may be able to take advantage of new tax laws, which may be less onerous than our current tax laws, or you may be in a lower tax bracket. Either way, you'll have more than if you pay tax on the money today and then grow it outside the tax-deductible, tax-deferred retirement account system we have today.

A GOOD START

Do you know what employer benefits are available to you? Many employees never really know how much their employer contributes to their retirement. Schedule an appointment with the human resources or benefits administrator who oversees your benefits, to have them explained to you. You may find that you're not taking full advantage of all the financially beneficial plans your employer offers, such as Cafeteria Plans for medical benefits (which allow you to use pre-tax dollars to pay for medical costs, like co-payments, dental visits, and eyeglasses), tuition waivers or reimbursements, or even public transportation subsidies (if you take the bus or train to work each day).

DON'T BORROW FROM YOUR RETIREMENT ACCOUNTS

A well-funded retirement account will give you comfort and security in your old age. But if you start borrowing from those accounts—even if you pay back the cash with interest—you'll lose out on some of the big benefits of compounding. But what should you do if you really need the money now?

The first thing to find out is whether your 401(k) or 403(b) program permits you to borrow from your accounts. Some do, some don't. Some 401(k) plans might allow you to borrow the cash for a short period of time, say five years. You must reimburse the plan for the principal borrowed, plus interest, or pay the 10-percent withdrawal penalty plus income taxes (because your loan will then be treated as a distribution for IRS purposes). In addition, if you leave the company while the cash is still outstanding, you may have to pay it off in full within thirty to sixty days of leaving, or the loan will again be treated as a distribution for IRS purposes. Check with your plan administrator for details.

Since the 1997 Tax Reform Act was passed, first-time home buyers are permitted to withdraw up to $10,000 from their conventional IRA or Roth IRA to pay for closing costs or the downpayment. You may also pay an unlimited amount of college expenses for yourself, your spouse, your children, or your grandchildren from your Roth IRA.

If you need cash, your retirement accounts should be the very last place you go for it. It's far better to refinance your home or take out a home-equity loan (the interest you pay is deductible), ask a friend or family member for a personal loan, or simply save up a reserve account that you can use for a down payment or any emergency that crops up. Remember, every dollar that doesn't grow on a tax-deductible and tax-deferred basis takes a whole lot longer to earn the same kind of return.

A GOOD START

Before you tap into your retirement program, try to find another place to get the money. And you should figure out how long you'll need the cash.

Although you don't want to take a cash advance on your credit card (ouch!), you might want to consider a home-equity loan, or refinancing your mortgage (if you own your home) to allow you to take out the cash that you need. You might also want to see if you can borrow the money from a relative (but put the loan in writing to protect both parties).

Reconsider why you need the cash. If you're paying off a credit-card debt, you might be better off tightening your belt and simply throwing every spare cent you have at the balance each month, rather than digging into your retirement cash, especially if you can transfer the balance to a cheaper card and throw the monthly savings into the pot as well.

START A PART-TIME BUSINESS
OUT OF YOUR HOME

It may surprise you to learn that the vast majority of businesses in this country are what are known as "mom and pop" shops. Many large businesses, especially in the technology world, often started as sideline projects out of a garage or a spare corner in the house. Women are actually starting home-based businesses far faster than men.

Pursuing a part-time business out of your home can ultimately turn into a full-blown career. Consider the paths these individuals have taken:

- Bruce, a chief technology officer for a telephone company, started a part-time consulting job on the side, and within two years he was consulting full-time. This gave him the opportunity to set his own hours, make more money, and spend all his time in the part of the business he enjoyed the most.

- Marcy worked as a sales and marketing manager for a Fortune 500 company before she was married. Once she had kids, she decided to be a stay-at-home mom. But as the kids grew older, she wanted to go back to work. She started helping her friends plan their weddings, special birthday celebrations, christenings, and bar mitzvahs. She was so good at it that word spread.

Now she rents office space and is doing corporate events for large companies, Web startups, and local municipalities. Her business will see sales in excess of $1 million this year.

- When Rick got laid off from his job, he started consulting for a variety of small businesses near where he worked while he looked for a full-time job. Suddenly, two of his clients offered him full-time positions. What began as a part-time job became a full-time job with part-time clients on the side.

- David works as a managing broker for a large real-estate firm. On the side, he buys multi-family buildings, renovates them, and then rents them out. He currently owns three buildings containing ten rental units, plus the building in which he lives. "This is my side business," he says. "It's what I do so that I can work for myself and ultimately have extra cash when I retire."

My own story is similar. I had left my previous job as a book editor, not knowing what I wanted to do. One of my authors, Phyllis, worked as a writer for the *Chicago Tribune*. She knew I'd written a few freelance pieces and suggested that I write additional pieces for the paper while I interviewed for a full-time job. In October 1988, I had four pieces published while I applied for more than two hundred jobs. By the end of the year I'd published nearly a dozen stories and I realized that I could make more money freelance writing than in my previous job. Also, I loved the freedom and flexibility that freelance writing offered. And so I started on my full-time writing career.

There's never been a better time to start a home-based business. The best thing about today's technology is that it allows you to run a small (or even a big) business right out of your spare bedroom, basement, or garage. With a computer, you can run Quicken or QuickBooks software (which can easily do the finances of a fairly substantial company), hook up to the Internet to do research on your competition and set up a Web site to sell your product or service, and create sales materials that will help you get the word out.

With an extra phone line or two, you can keep your business separate from your family finances, get set up to take payment through checks or credit cards, and keep in touch with your clients. Cell phones and pagers allow clients to contact you wherever you are in the world (even while on vacation, which may be the bad news). Laptop computers allow you to check your e-mail and keep in touch while on the road.

Don't know where to start? You can get help from the Small Business Administration (SBA.gov) on developing a business plan and finding financing. Your local chamber of commerce might run new-business seminars that will teach you some business basics and help you start your networking. You'll find more information about honing your idea on the Web, and can search there for competition.

Worried about getting into legal trouble because you're working from home? Many local governments are relaxing or eliminating their laws against home-based businesses. Check with your local municipality for details. Also, the IRS provides you with home-office deductions that might help you get your business off the ground.

While it requires some effort to get a home-based business up and running, the rewards (both mental and financial) can be huge. They have been for me, and I'm sure they will be for you.

A GOOD START

Think about what it is you like to do most. Do you like to sew? Paint? Write snappy copy? Create crafts projects? Dream up marketing campaigns? Take care of children? Cook? Bake? Are you a math whiz? What you need to do is look around at what you like to do, and figure out how to make money from it. If you have a large van, and young kids that you're constantly taking from one practice to another, perhaps you could start a business taking other kids to their lessons or practices. If you like to write, perhaps you can write for Web sites.

There are numerous low- and high-tech things you can do to make some money. All it takes is the time to formulate a plan and put it into action. For inspiration, check out the career section in your local library or bookstore and ask your friends about their jobs, professions, or hobbies. Start attending your local chamber of commerce meetings to network.

The ideas will come. Then it's up to you to take advantage of them.

TEN PERSONAL FINANCE MISTAKES YOU CAN'T AFFORD TO MAKE

When it comes to money, we all make mistakes. And, surely there are more than ten mistakes to be made. But if you're nimble, you'll not only avoid these mistakes, you'll probably avoid others as well.

1. Procrastinating. It's so much easier not to deal with serious issues like death, taxes, and money. Unfortunately, they're a part of life. Make a list of all your money chores and tackle the hardest one first, in the morning, when you're fresh and full of energy. Then move onto the easier tasks. You'll find that once you get the ball rolling, you'll have to run to keep up with it.

2. Spending more than you earn. If you want to be wealthy, you have to spend less than you earn. And then you have to invest your earnings wisely. It's that simple. If you live above your means, you'll always be in debt and you'll always be stressed about the fact that you're in debt. Debt weighs heavily, and can bring down the sunniest of souls. Don't let that be you.

3. Not saving enough. Most Americans save less than a half a percent of their annual income. Of those who do put away something, the majority have saved less than

$100,000. That isn't going to get you too far, particularly since most of us need anywhere from 80 percent to 120 percent of the annual income we were earning on the last day we worked. To get there, try to save twice what you think you'll need. What's the worst thing that can happen? You'll end up with too much money at a stage in your life when you have the time to enjoy it.

4. Overusing your credit cards. If you can afford to pay off your credit card in full at the end of the month, no matter how much you charge, then feel free to use that card as much as you like. Unfortunately, most of us can't afford to do that. And so, month after month, we continue to pay outrageous sums of interest (anywhere from 16 to 30 percent is common), none of which is deductible. If you're in debt up to your ears (other than mortgage debt), you'll never get ahead financially. So pay off all your non-deductible debt as quickly as possible.

5. Looking for the big kill. Yes, it's possible you will win the next $300-million Powerball lottery and collect more than enough money for several families to live on in style. But I wouldn't count on it. Nor would I count on picking a stock, putting everything I own into it, and counting on it soaring 2,000 percent in six months. If you're always looking for the big kill, you might miss out on some attractive but less aggressive investing opportunities that will, over time, significantly improve your personal finances.

6. Letting your emotions interfere with your investment strategy. Your investments are not your children, your parents, your best friends, or your pets; nor should they be your sole reason for living. But some folks get so caught up in the investment of the moment that they forget to check their emotions at the door. You want to manage your money with a cool head and plenty of research to back up that gut feeling.

7. Trying to time the market. No one can time the market. Even people who think they can time the market, who are paid millions of dollars each year by investment firms on Wall Street to do so, can't. If they can't do it, you can't either. The best way to invest in the stock market is by dollar-cost averaging—that is, investing the same amount each month, no matter what the market is doing. It's the safest and best way for most people to invest.

8. Failing to diversify your investments. The stock market goes up and the stock market goes down. And when it goes up and down over and over again within a short period, this is called market "volatility." The only way to keep yourself insulated is to invest in a wide range of companies in various market sectors, such as technology, energy, and telecommunications, that you can expect to move somewhat out of step with each other. The best reason to diversify: It'll let you sleep at night.

9. Chasing the investment "flavor of the month" (or week, day, or minute). Don't chase "hot" investments—or mutual-fund managers, for that matter. What you want to do is find solid companies and invest in them after you've thoroughly done your homework. Choose mutual funds that have good ten-year or fifteen-year track records. If they've performed well in the past, it's more likely they'll do well going forward.

10. Not taking enough risk. If the thought of taking risks keeps you awake at night, you'll need to temper those feelings. When it comes to investing, you'll need to take some risks or you'll never be able to grow your money. At best, you'll be able to keep it in a bank account that's FDIC-insured. Or, perhaps you'll invest in tax-free municipal bonds. But with risk comes reward in the stock market, the kind of gains that will keep you in cups of gourmet coffee throughout your retirement. The best time to take a risk is when you have twenty or thirty years until you retire, and a retirement account you can't touch. Start slowly, investing a little bit here and there until you get used to it, and then hang on for the ride. When it's all over, you'll probably have earned at least the 10-percent average annual return that the market has generated for the past seventy years—if not more.

WHERE TO GET
PROFESSIONAL HELP

If you decide you need professional help, here's a quick look at what kind of help is available and what it may cost you.

Financial Planners

There are three types of financial planners: commission-based planners, fee-only planners, and those that are a hybrid of both.

Commission-based planners take a commission on the assets you invest with them. So if you invest in a mutual fund with a 3 percent upfront load (a load is a commission you pay to the mutual fund), the planner will get a percentage of the load as his fee for recommending you. The planner will get a portion of the commission generated from each of the products and services he or she gets you to buy.

Fee-only planners typically charge clients on an hourly basis, or by the project. If they draw up a financial plan for you, the charge might come to $1,000 to $5,000, depending on the complexity of the plan. After that, consulting time may run $100 to $300 per hour. On the other hand, the fee-only planner isn't limited by commissions that are paid. So he or she isn't beholden to one group of investments or another. The field of investment choices is wide open. For consumers, fee-only planners are a good choice since you control how much money the planner will be paid, and there typically isn't an inherent conflict of interest (such as, the planner steering you to the products and services that pay him or her the highest commission).

The hybrid planners (half-commission, half-fee-only) charge less upfront, but will take a portion of the commission of products and services you are sold. Depending on the quality of the planner, and how much cash you have available to lay out, this may be an option for you. But beware of the hidden fees, and take a long, hard look at the rate of return of the investments over ten and twenty years. If you're going to pay a 5 percent load on anything—and I don't know why you would—you ought to have a good feeling that the investment will be good enough to compensate for the load over the long run. You should get concerned if the hybrid planner is pushing complicated investments (like limited partnerships), where the numbers are too tough for you to figure out. At that point, bail out and find someone else.

From time to time, you may run up against a financial planner who takes a percentage of your assets as a fee. For example, if you give the planner $100,000 and he or she takes 1 percent, you're paying $1,000 to have your money managed. This may be in addition to commissions earned on buying and selling securities. So be careful and ask lots of questions about how the planner will be paid.

Names of the Game

Financial planners often take different courses and exams to earn various designations that come after their names. For example, a stockbroker must pass exams in order to help you buy or sell securities (stocks, etc.). The basic tests are known as the Series 6 and Series 7 exams. Common planner credentials include Certified Financial Planner (CFP), Certified Fund Specialist (CFS), Chartered Mutual Fund Consultant (CMFC), or a Chartered Financial Analyst (CFA), which is among the best designation.

You may also find a planner who is a Certified Public Accountant (CPA), who has a Personal Financial Specialist (PFS) designation, or an Enrolled Agent (EA), which means that the individual has formerly worked for the IRS and is quite familiar with tax laws.

Anyone can hang out a shingle and call themselves a financial planner. You want someone who has put some time and study into earning at least some of these designations.

The ADV Form

Registered financial advisors must fill out a form known as the ADV-Advisors form. It is filed with securities regulators, and clients may ask to see both the first and second parts of the form.

The first part of the form deals with the advisor's disciplinary history. If there's ever been trouble, if the advisor has been suspended, fined, or otherwise disciplined, it should be listed on the form. Needless to say, if there's trouble listed, find another advisor. The second part of the form details how the advisor is paid for his or her services. You should ask to see both parts of the ADV form. If the planner balks at showing you, simply cut your losses and find another planner.

You can always check on a planner's or stockbroker's ADV by calling the National Association of Securities Dealers (NASD) public disclosure hotline (800-289-9999).

Finding a Planner

The following organizations offer referrals to planners, but they don't necessarily guarantee that you'll get good results. So be sure to check out the planner thoroughly and talk to current clients:

Financial Planning Association (800-282-PLAN). Web site: www.FPANET.org. Free publication: *How a Financial Planner Can Help You and How to Choose the Right One.*

National Association of Personal Financial Advisors, a trade group of fee-only financial advisors (888-FEE-ONLY). Free publication: *Why Select a Fee-Only Financial Advisor.*

American Institute of Certified Public Accounts (888-777-7077). You can request a recommendation to a CPA who is also a Personal Financial Specialists. Web site: www.cpapfs.org.

Finding a Tax Advisor or Enrolled Agent

National Association of Enrolled Agents (EA) (800-424-4339). Web site: www.naea.org. These individuals are able to represent individuals and corporations before the IRS.

American Institute of Certified Public Accountants (CPA) (212/596-6200). To find a CPA in your area, call your state CPA society. Web site: www.aicpa.org.

A GUIDE TO COMMONLY USED FINANCIAL TERMS

Abstract (of Title)   A summary of the public records affecting the title to a particular piece of land. An attorney or title insurance company officer creates the abstract of title by examining all recorded instruments (documents) relating to a specific piece of property, such as easements, liens, mortgages, etc.

Accelerated Benefit   A rider that allows a terminally ill person to cash in a policy before he or she dies, and collect up to 95 percent of the policy's face value (the benefit amount stated on the policy).

Acceleration Clause   A provision in a loan agreement that allows the lender to require the balance of the loan to become due immediately if mortgage payments are not made or there is a breach in your obligation under your mortgage or note.

Accumulation Fund   The savings component of a universal life insurance policy. The money in this fund earns interest and goes to pay the higher cost of the mortality charge as you age. As long as you pay enough to fund the mortality charge, you can skip payments if your funds dry up. And if you contribute enough to the accumulation fund early on and you get a few good years of interest, that interest may be enough to pay the premium later on.

Acquisition or Bank Fee   The average fee you'll pay to a car dealer at the start of a car lease. Typically it is $300 to $400, and is not negotiable.

Addendum   Any addition to, or modification of, a contract. Also called an *amendment* or *rider*.

Adjustable-Rate Mortgage (ARM)   A type of loan whose prevailing interest rate is tied to an economic index which fluctuates with the market. The three most popular types of ARMs are one-year ARMs, which adjust every year, three-year ARMs, which adjust every three years, and five-year ARMs, which adjust every five years. When the loan adjusts, the lender tacks a margin onto the economic index rate to come up with your loan's new rate. ARMs are considered riskier than fixed-rate mortgages, but their starting interest rates are generally lower than a longer-term rate, and in the past five to ten years people have done very well with them.

Adjusted Gross Income   Your total income reduced by contributions to retirement accounts, alimony payments, and certain other exclusions, or other "items."

Agency   A term used to describe the relationship between a home seller and a real-estate broker, or a home buyer and a real-estate broker.

Agency Closing   The lender's use of a title company or other party to act on the lender's behalf for the purposes of closing on the purchase of a home or refinancing of a home loan.

Agent   An individual who acts on behalf of a consumer. A real-estate agent represents a buyer or a seller in the purchase or sale of a home. Licensed by the state, a real-estate agent must work for a broker or a brokerage firm. An insurance agent helps a consumer purchase an insurance policy. Insurance agents are also licensed by the state.

Agreement of Sale   This document is also known as the contract of purchase, purchase agreement, or sales agreement. It is the agreement by which the seller agrees to sell you his or her property if you pay a certain price. It contains all the provisions and conditions for the purchase, must be written, and is signed by both parties.

Amortization   A payment plan that enables the borrower to repay his debt gradually through monthly payments of principal and interest. Amortization tables allow you to see exactly how much you pay each month in interest and how much you repay in principal, depending on the amount of money borrowed at a specific interest rate.

Annual Mileage Allowance   The number of miles included as part of a car lease. Car dealers will offer as few miles as they can get away with, perhaps as few as 10,000 per year, or 30,000 over a three-year lease. But they will go as high as 15,000 miles per year if you negotiate it. You'll pay anywhere from ten cents to fifty cents for each additional mile you drive over the limit, so think carefully about how far you drive every year, and negotiate carefully.

Annual Percentage Rate (APR)   The total cost of a loan, expressed as a percentage rate of interest, which not only includes the loan's interest rate, but factors in all the costs associated with making that loan, including closing costs and fees. The costs are then amortized over the life of the loan. Banks are required by the federal truth-in-lending statutes to disclose the APR of a loan, which gives borrowers a way to compare various loans from different lenders.

Any-Occupation Policy   A type of private disability insurance that pays if—from the insurer's perspective—you can't work at any job for which your education and training qualify you.

Application Fee   A one-time fee charged by a company for processing your application for a loan. For a home loan, the application fee is sometimes applied toward certain costs, including the appraisal and credit report.

Appraisal   The opinion of an appraiser, who estimates the value of a home at a specific point in time for the purpose of financing or refinancing a home.

Articles-of-Agreement for Deed   A type of seller financing that allows the buyer to purchase a home in installments over a specified period. The seller keeps legal title to the home until the loan is paid off. The buyer receives an interest in the property—called equitable title—but does not own it. Because the buyer is paying the real-estate taxes and paying interest to the seller, however, it is the buyer who receives the tax benefits of home ownership.

Asset Allocation   A term used to express your choice among different types of asset classes and styles. You might have growth or value funds, which are mutual funds typically focused on companies that are growing quickly, or companies that are perhaps out of favor temporarily, and are typically priced cheaply relative to their assets, profits, and potential. Value funds are betting that these stocks have a lot of room to grow. Your fund may be international (holding shares of international companies) or domestic (holding shares of U.S. companies only). It might be large-cap (focused on huge corporations), mid-cap (medium-sized companies), or small-cap (smaller companies).

Assumption of Mortgage   If you assume a mortgage when you purchase a home, you undertake to fulfill the obligations of the existing loan agreement the seller made with the lender. The obligations are similar to those that you would incur if you took out a new mortgage. When assuming a mortgage, you become personally liable for the payment of principal and interest. The seller, or original mortgagor, should be released from the liability, and should get that release in writing. Otherwise he or she could be liable if you don't make the monthly payments.

Balloon Mortgage   A type of mortgage that is generally short in length, but is amortized over twenty-five or thirty years so that the borrower pays a combination of interest and principal each month. At the end of the loan term, the entire balance of the loan must be repaid at once.

Blue Chips   Large, well-established companies that offer investors some growth with a solid dividend. Companies listed on the S&P 500 are frequently referred to as blue-chip stocks, capable of weathering even the worst market fluctuations.

Bond   A government's (federal or municipal) or a corporation's obligation to repay you your principal plus a certain amount of interest over a fixed period.

Bond Fund   A mutual fund made up of bond issues.

Broker, Real Estate   An individual who acts as the agent of the seller or buyer. A real-estate broker must be licensed by the state.

Broker, Stock   An individual who helps consumers purchase equities, such as stocks and bonds. A stockbroker must be licensed.

Building Line or Setback   The distance from the front, back, or side of a lot beyond which construction or improvements may not extend without permission by the proper governmental authority or other party. The building line may be established by a filed plat of subdivision, by restrictive covenants in deeds, by building codes, or by zoning ordinances.

Buy-Down   An incentive offered by a developer or home seller that allows the homebuyer to lower his or her initial interest rate by putting up a certain amount of money. Also the process of paying extra points up front at the closing of your loan in order to have a lower interest rate over the life of the loan.

Buyer Broker   A buyer broker is a real-estate broker who specializes in representing buyers. Unlike a seller broker or conventional broker, the buyer broker has a fiduciary duty to the buyer, because the buyer accepts the legal obligation of paying the broker. The buyer broker is obligated to find the best property for a client and then negotiate the best possible purchase price and terms. Buyer brokerage has gained a significant amount of respect in recent years, since the National Association of Realtors has changed its code of ethics to accept this designation.

Buyer's Market   Conditions that favor the buyer. A buyer's market usually occurs when there are too many homes for sale, and a home can be bought for less money.

Call   An order issued by a company to its preferred stock or bond holders to turn in their stock or bonds for money.

Callability   The condition whereby a bond may be called in before it is due. This means the issuer of the bond may decide to refinance its debt and pay back all of the bond holders early. If interest rates fall, the chances of a bond being called increase because the bond holder could simply refinance the debt for less money (just as you'd refinance your mortgage if rates dropped).

Capital Gain   A profit made on the sale of stocks, bonds, real estate, or other assets.

Capitalized Cost (or Gross Capitalized Cost) The price of the car that the dealer uses to construct the lease. It also includes all the features and services that come with the car in the lease. A crucial number, it is negotiable.

Capitalized Cost Reduction Your down payment for the purchase of a car. It is negotiable. If you're trading in a car, the value of the trade-in should be applied to either the capitalized cost reduction or your monthly payments.

Capital Loss The loss taken on the sale of stocks, bonds, real estate, or other assets.

Certificate of Title A document or instrument issued by a local government agency to an owner, naming the owner as the owner of an automobile or boat. When the item is sold, the certificate of title is transferred to the buyer. The agency then issues a new certificate of title to the buyer.

Cash Surrender Value (Cash Value) The amount available in cash upon voluntary termination of an insurance policy by its owner before it becomes payable by death or maturity. This amount is typically paid in cash or paid-up insurance.

Cash Value Policy A category of life insurance including whole life, universal life, and variable universal life that combines the death benefit with a savings component. The insurance policy is broken down into two parts: the mortality charge (the part that pays for the death benefit) and a reserve (the savings component that earns interest). As you get older, the cost of the death benefit rises. In addition to interest, the reserve might receive an annual dividend, depending on how many policies have been paid out, and how well the insurer has invested the premiums it has received.

Catastrophic Care   Most health insurance policies cover catastrophic care, including such procedures as transplants, complex neonatal care, severe burns care, or trauma care.

Chain of Title   The lineage of ownership of a particular property.

Churning   Also known as twisting, churning is an attempt by an unscrupulous agent from an insurance company to cancel your existing policy and replace it with a new one, drawing down your cash value (called "juice" in industry jargon) to pay for it. This activity generates additional commission for the agent and may result in your having to pay more down the line. It is also a word used to describe the actions of a stockbroker who continually buys and sells for an account. Churning profits for the broker often eat up whatever profits might be there for the consumer.

Classified Shares   Mutual fund shares grouped alphabetically. "A" shares are traditional "load" funds where you pay the broker right off the top of your investment. "B" shares still pay a commission, but the mutual fund puts up the money and then gradually withdraws it from your account. "C" and "D" shares are sometimes called level-load funds. The broker gets no commission up front, but instead gets an annual fee (called a trail commission) from the investor's account.

Closed-Ended   A mutual fund that has closed its doors to new investors and their cash in order to maintain its size and position in the market.

Closing   The final piece of a home purchase or sale when cash or other considerations is exchanged for the deed to the property.

Code-and-Condition Coverage (Building Code Coverage)   A homeowner's insurance rider that covers the cost of meeting new building codes that may have gone into effect after a home was built and to which any new homes built are subject. Also known as an ordinance-and-law rider.

Common Stock   A share of ownership in a company.

Conditionally Renewable Policy   A type of private disability insurance policy that may be renewed at the insurer's discretion.

Consumer Federation of America (CFA)   A nonprofit association of consumer interest groups that works to further the consumer interest through educational programs and advocacy. The CFA pays particular attention to those in need, including children, elderly persons living on fixed incomes, and the poor.

Consumer Price Index (CPI)   A measure of the changes in price of many of the goods and services that urban households purchase for consumption. The CPI is used as an economic indicator, a policy guide, a means to adjust income payments for inflation, and a means to determine the cost of school lunches, to mention a few of its uses.

Contrarian Fund   A stock mutual fund that is positioned against conventional wisdom. When Asia was headed into a recession during the late 1990s, contrarian international funds went in and began swooping up the stocks of companies, betting that they'd come back.

Convertible Bond   A bond that can be converted into shares of stock in a corporation.

Corporate Bond   A bond issued by a corporation.

Cost-Of-Living Adjustments (COLA)   A rider that can be added to a long-term-care policy under which the policy owner's benefits increase to keep pace with the consumer price index (CPI).

Coupon   The actual interest payment made on each bond. If you have a $5,000 bond paying 7 percent interest, you will receive $350 each year, most likely in two $175 payments. The $350 is the coupon. The interest rate of the bond is also referred to as the *coupon rate*. The name originates from how investors used to collect their interest (and still do on some). They would actually clip a coupon and bring it in to receive the interest. Today this is often done electronically, with the interest simply deposited in one's bank account.

Current Yield   The coupon interest payment divided by the bond's price. This will fluctuate based on where interest rates are, and what you could currently sell your bond for in the marketplace.

Debt Service   The total amount of debt (credit cards, mortgage, car loan) that an individual is carrying at any one time.

Deferred Compensation Plan   Employees may put a limited portion of their pre-tax earnings into a deferred compensation plan, like a 401(k) or a Keogh. The earnings are excluded from tax calculations and grow tax-free until the funds are withdrawn at retirement.

Dependent   An individual for whom the taxpayer provides over half of the support for the calendar year. This could be a child, spouse, relative, or nonrelative living as a member of the taxpayer's household.

Discount   Newly issued bonds are typically sold at some sort of discount. A bond that has a face value of $1,000 and sells for $925 has a $75 discount. When interest rates rise, bonds are discounted more because a less expensive bond is needed to achieve the same interest rate.

Diversified Funds   According to the Diversified Mutual Fund Investment Act of 1940, a mutual fund calling itself diversified must have 75 percent of its assets divided up so no more than 5 percent of the fund's assets are invested in a single stock. Funds that do not call themselves diversified may invest a larger portion of their holdings in a single stock.

Dividends   A shareholder's share of a company's profits, typically paid out in quarterly installments. To find out how much you'll receive, multiply the dividend (published in your local paper) by the number of shares you own.

Endorsement   An amendment to an insurance policy, usually by means of a rider.

Equity   Your share of ownership in a company. Stockholders are often referred to as equity investors, because they invest in the equity of a company.

Escrow   A third-party account in which monies are held. For example, a lender would set up an escrow account to pay a property's insurance premiums and tax bill. Or, a good faith deposit would be held in an escrow account until the transaction has closed.

Estimated Tax Payments   If you are self-employed or have significant dividend income or investment income in addition to your regular salary, you must make tax payments based on the estimated tax you'll owe at the end of the year. Your estimated tax payments must equal either 100 percent of the tax you paid in the previous year, or 90 percent of your total tax for the current year.

Exemption (Tax)   You may take a tax exemption from your adjusted gross income for yourself, your spouse, and any dependents. The tax exemption basically excludes money from taxation.

Fee Simple   The most basic type of ownership, under which the owner has the right to use and dispose of a property at will.

Fiduciary Duty   A relationship of trust between a broker and a seller, a buyer broker and a buyer, or an attorney and a client.

Filing Status   A declaration as to your personal status (i.e., married, single, separated, having dependents or not). Your filing status will determine your standard deduction, the tax rate table you'll use to compute your tax liability, and the deductions and credits to which you're entitled.

First Mortgage   A mortgage that takes priority over all other voluntary liens.

Fixture   Personal property, such as built-in bookcases, furnaces, hot water heaters, and recessed lights, that becomes "affixed" because it has been permanently attached to the home.

Foreclosure   The legal action taken to extinguish a homeowner's right and interest in a property, so that the property can be sold in a foreclosure sale to satisfy a debt.

401(k)   A defined contribution plan for employees. Some companies do not offer this benefit, but if they do, you may contribute up to a maximum set by the government and indexed to inflation. As an additional benefit, some employers match contributions up to a certain dollar limit or percentage.

403(b)   A retirement plan offered by certain religious, charitable, or public organizations. It operates much like a 401(k) plan.

Fund of Funds   A mutual fund that is made up of other mutual funds. The idea here is that if you think you're not diversified enough in choosing a diversified mutual fund, you buy one fund that diversifies by purchasing several different funds.

Fund Supermarket   A relatively new concept, a fund supermarket is an investment firm (often called a family) that offers not only its own mutual funds, but the ability to invest in the mutual funds of other families. The nice thing about this is that all of your investments in these funds are displayed on one statement from your primary family. On the downside, sometimes supermarkets tack on additional charges for investing in a fund outside the family if that fund doesn't pay a commission separately.

GAP Insurance   This stands for "guaranteed auto protection," and you need it if you're leasing. This insurance will pay the balance on the lease and the early termination penalties if the car is stolen or totaled. Negotiate to have it included with your lease payment.

Gift Letter   A letter to the lender indicating that a gift of cash has been made to the buyer and that it is not expected to be repaid. The letter must detail the amount of the gift and the name of the giver.

Good Faith Estimate (GFE)   Under the Real Estate Settlement Procedures Act, or RESPA, lenders are required to give potential borrowers a written good faith estimate of closing costs within three days of an application submission.

Grace Period   The period after a loan payment due date in which a mortgage payment may be made and not be considered delinquent.

Graduated Payment Mortgage   A mortgage in which the payments increase over the life of the mortgage, allowing the borrower to make very low payments at the beginning of the loan.

Growth Stock   A company that is focusing on growing above all else. All profits are typically reinvested into the company to keep it growing quickly, so little if any dividends are paid.

Guaranteed Cost Replacement Insurance   A type of homeowner's insurance that guarantees to rebuild your home no matter what the cost, and has a rider built in to take care of inflation. On some policies, insurers might only pay to rebuild your home up to 120 to 125 percent of your policy amount. It's up to you to stay on top of how much it will cost to rebuild your home.

Guaranteed Renewable Policy   An insurance policy that must be renewed as long as the insured pays the premium on time. Typically, an insurer cannot make any changes to a guaranteed renewable policy other than to increase the premium rate for an entire class of policyholders.

Hard Asset Funds   A mutual fund that holds a portion of its assets in gold or silver or other commodities like these, or in indices that are based on hard assets. Hard asset funds may also be invested in real estate.

Hazard Insurance   Insurance that covers the property from damages that might materially affect its value. Also known as homeowner's insurance.

Health Insurance Portability and Accountability Act   Effective July 1, 1997, this act specifies that if a person has been covered by insurance during the past twelve months, a new insurer cannot refuse to cover that person, nor can it force him or her to accept a waiting period when joining a new group plan.

HMO (Health Maintenance Organization)   An organization that provides a wide range of comprehensive health-care services for a specified group at a fixed periodic payment. An HMO can be sponsored by the government, medical schools, hospitals, employers, labor unions, consumer groups, insurance companies, and hospital-medical plans.

Holdback   An amount of money held back at closing by the lender or the escrow agent until a particular condition has been met. If the problem is a repair, the money is kept until the repair is made. If the repair is not made, the lender or escrow agent uses the money to make the repair. Buyers and sellers may also have holdbacks between them, to ensure that specific conditions of the sale are met.

Homeowner's Association   A group of homeowners in a particular subdivision or area who band together to take care of common property and common interests.

Homeowner's Insurance   Coverage that includes hazard insurance, as well as personal liability and theft.

Home Warranty   A service contract that covers appliances (with exclusions) in working condition in the home for a certain period, usually one year. Homeowners are responsible for a per-call service fee. There is a homeowner's warranty for new construction. Some developers will purchase a warranty from a company specializing in new construction for the homes they sell. A homeowner's warranty will warrant the good working order of the appliances and workmanship of a new home for between one and ten years; for example, appliances might be covered for one year, while the roof may be covered for several years.

Hostile Takeover   This occurs when a company purchases another against the will of the purchased company's management.

Housing and Urban Development, Department of   Also known as HUD, this is the federal department responsible for the nation's housing programs. It also regulates

RESPA, the Real Estate Settlement Procedures Act, which governs how lenders must deal with their customers.

Inception Fees   These are the up-front fees that a car dealer will require you to pay, including your first monthly payment, refundable security deposit, Department of Motor Vehicle (DMV) fees, and possibly an acquisition fee. You'll have to come up with this cash up front, even if you're getting a "no money down" lease. If you're paying a down payment, you'll have to add that in as well.

Income Replacement Policy   A category of private disability insurance that covers the difference between what you earned prior to the disability and what you now earn doing a different job.

Income Stock   A company that tends to pay out more of its profits to shareholders (in the form of dividends) and put less toward growth.

Indemnity Plans   A type of health-care insurance set up as a fee-for-service plan. Typically there are no restrictions on care, and the plan coverage kicks in when you reach a certain deductible. Unlike an HMO, you (or the doctor's office) will also have to bill the insurance company. The nice thing about indemnity plans is that you can see the doctor you choose and seek second opinions or specialists anywhere in the country. On the other hand, it's the most expensive way to go, and not every employer offers this plan.

Index Funds   These are stock mutual funds designed to mimic the movements of a particular index. For example, a fund trying to mimic the movement of the Standard & Poor's (S&P) 500 will either purchase every stock on the S&P 500 in the same ratio that those stocks appear on the index, or will purchase a representative sample of companies that closely approximate the index. Since index funds rarely change their holdings, they are typically cheap to hold, and may do better for investors over the long haul.

Individual Retirement Account (IRA)   An account to which any individual who earns income may contribute up to $2,000 per year. The contributions are tax-deductible, and the earnings grow tax-free, although they may be taxed upon withdrawal.

Initial Public Offering (IPO)   A young company hoping to finance future growth will often go public to raise additional funds. Many IPOs rise dramatically the first day of the offering, then settle back down to a more reasonable share price. Some investors try to get in on the ground floor of an IPO, and then sell their shares within the first day or week.

Inspection, Home   The service a professional home inspector performs when he or she is hired to scrutinize a house for any possible structural defects, typically done in advance of a closing. May also be done in order to check for the presence of toxic substances, such as leaded paint or water, asbestos, radon, or pests, including termites.

Installment Contract for Deed   The purchase of property in installments. Title to the property is given to the purchaser when all installments are made.

Institutional Investors or Lenders   Private or public companies, corporations, or funds (such as pension funds) that purchase loans on the secondary market from commercial lenders such as banks or savings and loans. They may also be sources of funds for mortgages through mortgage brokers.

Interest   Money charged for the use of borrowed funds. Usually expressed as an interest rate, it is the percentage of the total loan charged annually for the use of the funds.

Interest-Only Mortgage   A loan in which only the interest is paid on a regular basis (usually monthly), and the principal is owed in full at the end of the loan term. The advantage to an interest-only loan is that you can borrow a larger amount of money and write off everything you pay the lender. The disadvantage is that you do not build up any equity as you pay off the loan each month.

Interest Rate Cap   The total number of percentage points that an adjustable-rate mortgage (ARM) is allowed to rise over the life of the loan.

Joint Tenancy   An equal, undivided ownership in a property taken by two or more owners. Under joint tenancy, there are rights of survivorship, which means that if one of the owners dies, the surviving owner, rather than the heirs of the estate, inherits the other's total interest in the property.

Keogh   A retirement plan for employees of unincorporated businesses or self-employed individuals. You may contribute up to 25 percent of your earned income, to a maximum of $30,000.

Landscape   The trees, flowers, plantings, lawn, and shrubbery that surround the exterior of a dwelling.

Late Charge   A penalty applied to a mortgage payment that arrives after the grace period (usually the tenth or fifteenth of a month).

Lease Charge or Money Factor   This is the complicated way car dealers calculate lease payments. Similar to an interest rate, multiply the money factor by 2,400 to approximate the annual percentage rate of your lease. It is not negotiable, but differs from lease to lease, from car to car, and from company to company. Usually it is not disclosed, because car companies are not required to do so under Regulation M (see below).

Lease with an Option to Buy   A lease according to which the renter or lessee of a piece of property has the right to purchase the property for a specific period at a specific price. Usually a lease with an option to buy allows a first-time buyer to accumulate a down payment by applying a portion of the monthly rent toward the down payment.

Lender   A person, company, corporation, or entity that lends money for the purchase of real estate.

Lessee   The person leasing a vehicle or residence (known as a tenant).

Lessor   The landlord or leasing company, bank, or finance company that leases a car or other property to the lessee.

Letter of Intent   A formal statement, usually in letter form, from the buyer to the seller stating that the buyer intends to purchase a specific piece of property for a specific price on a specific date.

Leverage   The use of a small amount of cash, such as a 10- or 20-percent down payment, to purchase a piece of property.

Lien   An encumbrance against a property, which may be voluntary or involuntary. There are many different kinds of liens, including a tax lien (for unpaid federal, state, or real-estate taxes), a judgment lien (for monetary judgments by a court of law), a mortgage lien (when you take out a mortgage), and a mechanic's lien (for work done by a contractor that has not been paid for). For a lien to be attached to the property's title, it must usually be filed or recorded with a local county government office.

Life Cycle Fund   A mutual fund designed specifically to mirror what many experts feel are optimum ratios of stocks and bonds throughout the different stages in the investor's life. You may be able to choose from three or four funds, ones designed for twenty-to-thirty-year-olds, ones for forty-to-fifty-year-olds, and so on.

Listing   A property that a broker agrees to list for sale in return for a commission.

Load   A sales charge on a mutual fund that can range from 1 to 7 percent. It might be a front-load (payable when you buy into the fund) or a back-load (payable when you cash out). You typically pay this because you want the service of a financial professional selecting and building your portfolio. Your load may decrease the longer you hold the fund. If you cashed out in the first year, you'd pay 6 percent. If you cash out three years later, the load may be only 3 percent.

Loan   An amount of money that is lent to a borrower, who agrees to repay it plus interest.

Loan Commitment   A written document that states that a mortgage company has agreed to lend a buyer a certain amount of money at a certain rate of interest for a specific period. The loan commitment may contain sets of conditions and a date by which the loan must close.

Loan Origination Fee   A one-time fee charged by a mortgage company to arrange the financing for a loan.

Loan-to-Value Ratio   The ratio of the amount of money you wish to borrow compared to the value of the property you wish to purchase. Institutional investors (who buy loans on the secondary market from mortgage companies) set up certain ratios that guide lending practices. For example, the mortgage company might only lend you 80 percent of a property's value.

Location   Where property is geographically situated. "Location, location, location" is a broker's maxim that states that where a building is located is its most important feature, because you can change virtually everything about it except its location.

Lock-In   The mechanism by which a borrower locks in the interest rate that will be charged on a particular loan. Usually the lock lasts for a certain time period, such as thirty, forty-five, or sixty days. On a loan for a home under construction, the lock-in may be much longer.

Long-Term-Care Insurance   Insurance that covers the cost of long-term care in a nursing home, in other custodial care settings, or at home.

Maintenance Fee   The monthly or annual fee charged to condo, co-op, or townhouse owners, and paid to the homeowner's association for the maintenance of common property. Also called an *assessment*.

Management Buyout   When the individuals running a company get together, borrow money, and buy most or all of its common shares.

Market Price   On any given day, your bond will be worth more or less than the face value. That's because the bond market is continually active, with traders bidding up and down the value of bonds based on the current interest rate of the day. When interest rates rise, bonds are worth less (because it takes a smaller amount of capital to earn the same amount of interest). When interest rates fall, bonds are worth more (because it takes a greater amount of money to earn the same amount of interest).

Market Sector   The categorizing of companies based on the industry in which they operate. Some sectors include technology and transportation.

Matured Bond   A bond that has been paid back in full, or is due for full payment.

Medicaid   State public assistance programs to persons who are unable to pay for health care. Title XIX of the federal Social Security Act provides matching federal funds for financing state Medicaid programs.

Medicare   A program of Hospital Insurance (Part A) and Supplementary Medical Insurance (Part B) protection provided under the Social Security Act.

Medicare Supplemental Insurance (Medigap or Med-Sup)   A term used in reference to private insurance products that supplement Medicare insurance benefits.

Merger   This occurs when two companies voluntarily join together. Sometimes mergers are really takeovers in which one company ends up becoming the dominant presence.

Mortgage   A document granting a lien on a home in exchange for financing granted by a lender. The mortgage is the means by which the lender secures the loan and has the ability to foreclose on the home.

Mortgage Banker   A company or a corporation, such as a bank, that lends its funds to borrowers in addition to bringing together lenders and borrowers. A mortgage banker may also service the loan (i.e., collect the monthly payments).

Mortgage Broker   A company or individual that brings together lenders and borrowers and processes mortgage applications.

Mortgagee   A legal term for the lender.

Mortgagor   A legal term for the borrower.

Multiple Listing Service (MLS)   A computerized listing of all properties offered for sale by member brokers. Buyers may only gain access to the MLS by working with a member broker.

Municipal Bond   A bond offered by a local municipality. "Munis," as they are commonly known, are not taxed by the federal government.

Negative Amortization   A condition created when the monthly mortgage payment is less than the amount necessary to pay off the loan over the period set forth in the note. Because you're paying less than the amount necessary, the actual loan amount increases over time. That's how you end up with negative equity. To pay off the loan, a lump-sum payment may have to be made.

Net Asset Value (NAV)   The value per share of a mutual fund. This is similar to a stock price.

No-Fault Insurance   A legal policy adopted by some states that abolishes liability for a death or injury caused by a motor vehicle, regardless of the accident's cause. An injured party cannot sue another driver unless a particular crime or hazard is proven. Drivers in states with no-fault insurance laws can buy *personal injury protection*, which means you pay for your injuries and the other driver pays for his or her injuries.

No-Load   Mutual funds that charge no fees to buy in or cash out. There are other charges, however. Check the fund's *expense ratio* to find out how much you're being charged.

Non-Cancelable Policy   A policy specifying that as long as you pay your premiums on time, the insurer can't raise your premium and can't cancel your policy.

Open-Ended   This describes a mutual fund that continues to welcome new investors and their cash.

Open-End Lease   When you bring the car back, the dealer compares the actual value of the car with the residual value stated in your lease contract. If the actual value is less than the stated residual value, you make up the difference. If, by chance, the car has retained more than its residual value, the dealer pays you.

Operating Expense Ratio (OER)   Also known as the expense ratio, the OER is the cost of administering and managing a mutual fund, including salaries and bonuses paid. The ratio can run .05 to 3 percent per year.

Option to Purchase   Also known as a lease/option, this occurs when a buyer pays for the right or option to purchase property for a given length of time, without having the obligation to actually purchase the property.

Optionally Renewable Policy   A contract of health insurance in which the insurer reserves the right to terminate the coverage at any anniversary or, in some cases, at any premium due date, but does not have the right to terminate coverage between such dates.

Ordinance-and-Law Rider   See *Code-and-Condition Coverage*

Origination Fee   A fee charged by the lender for allowing you to borrow money to purchase property. The fee—which is also referred to as *points*—is usually expressed as a percentage of the total loan amount.

Ownership   The absolute right to use, enjoy, and dispose of property. You own it!

Own-Occupation Policy   A type of private disability insurance that pays if you can't work at your specific job.

Package Mortgage   A mortgage that uses both real and personal property to secure a loan.

Paper   Jargon that refers to the mortgage, trust deed, installment, and land contract.

Par   A bond's face value. A $1,000 bond will have a par value of $1,000. The term may be a bit confusing because even if your bond is worth $10,000, par also refers to 100, as in 100 percent of a bond's value. So you may hear that your bond cost 95, which means 95 percent of par. That means you'll get a 5-percent discount, and pay $950 for every bond with a $1,000 face value. If the bond cost 116, that means it's 116 percent of par, or cost you $1,160 for a bond with a face value of $1,000.

Partial Disability Coverage   A benefit sometimes found in disability income policies providing for the payment of reduced monthly income in the event the insured cannot work full-time and/or is prevented from performing one or more important daily duties pertaining to his or her occupation.

Penalty (IRS)   A fine levied by the IRS. You may pay a flat dollar fee or a fee based on an interest charge for unpaid taxes, failure to pay taxes, failure to make estimated tax payments, failure to make federal tax deposits, or filing late.

Personal Articles Rider   Coverage designed to insure property of a movable nature. The coverage typically protects against all physical loss, subject to special exclusions and conditions.

Personal Injury Protection   First-party no-fault coverage in which an insurer pays, within the specified limits, the wage loss, medical, hospital, and funeral expenses of the insured.

Personal Property   Movable property, such as appliances, furniture, clothing, and artwork.

PITI   An acronym for "principal, interest, taxes, and insurance." These are usually the four parts of your monthly mortgage payment.

Pledged Account   Borrowers who do not want to have a real-estate tax or insurance escrow administered by the mortgage servicer can, in some circumstances, pledge a savings account into which enough money to cover real-estate taxes and the insurance premium must be deposited. You must then make the payments for your real-estate taxes and insurance premiums from a separate account. If you fail to pay your taxes or premiums, the lender is allowed to use the funds in the pledged account to make those payments.

Point   A point is 1 percent of the loan amount.

POS (Point of Service) Plan   A health insurance plan that permits an individual to choose providers outside the plan yet encourages the use of network providers. This type of plan is also known as an open-ended HMO or PPO.

Possession   Being in control of a piece of property, and having the right to use it to the exclusion of all others.

Power of Attorney   The legal authorization given to an individual to act on behalf of another individual.

PPO (Preferred Provider Organization)   An arrangement whereby a third-party payer contracts with a group of medical care providers who furnish services at lower-than-usual fees in return for prompt payment and a certain volume of patients.

Preexisting Condition   A physical condition that existed before the effective date of coverage.

Preferred Stock   A special class of stock that may have certain voting privileges. Companies typically pay a fixed high dividend whose return is similar to what you'd get on a bond. While the price of preferred stock can rise, common stock prices typically rise faster than preferred stock.

Prepaid Interest   Interest paid at closing for the number of days left in the month after closing. For example, if you close on the fifteenth, you would prepay the interest for the fifteenth through the end of the month.

Prepayment Penalty   A fine imposed when a loan is paid off before it comes due. Many states now have laws against prepayment penalties, although banks with federal charters claim to be exempt from state laws. If possible, do not use a mortgage that has a prepayment penalty, or you will be charged a fine if you sell your property before your mortgage has been paid off.

Prequalifying for a Loan   This occurs when a mortgage company tells a buyer in advance of the formal application approximately how much money the buyer can afford to borrow.

Presumptive Disability   A type of private disability insurance that presumes its holder to be fully disabled and entitled to full benefits if he or she loses his or her sight, speech, hearing, or some other specified faculty.

Price-to-Earnings Ratio (P/E)   This is the price of a stock divided by a company's earnings per share. Typically, newspapers will publish a company's P/E ratio in the stock market tables. When a company's stock has a high P/E ratio, its earnings may be low while the price of the stock is high.

Principal   If you're getting a home loan, the principal is the amount of money you borrow. If you're buying a bond, the principal is the amount you're lending. Typically, you'll buy bonds with a face value of $1,000. If you buy a $1,000 bond, your principal is $1,000.

Private Mortgage Insurance (PMI)   Special insurance that specifically protects the top 20 percent of a loan, allowing the lender to lend more than 80 percent of the value of the property. PMI is paid in monthly installments by the borrower, and is for the benefit of the lender, not the buyer.

Property Tax   A tax levied by a county or local authority on the value of real estate.

Proration   The proportional division of certain costs of home ownership. Usually used at closing to figure out how much the buyer and seller each owe for certain expenditures, including real-estate taxes, assessments, and water bills.

Purchase Agreement   An agreement between the buyer and seller for the purchase of property.

Purchase Fee   A fee you'll pay in addition to the purchase option price if you decide to purchase your leased car at the end of the lease term. Typically, it's about $250–$300, and it is negotiable.

Purchase Money Mortgage   An instrument used in seller financing, a purchase money mortgage is signed by a buyer and given to the seller in exchange for a portion of the purchase price.

Purchase-Option Price   The price you'll pay to buy a car at the end of a lease. Typically, it's not negotiable, but it may be tied into the number of miles you're allotted each year. A car that's driven 15,000 miles a year will be less valuable than a car driven only 10,000 miles a year.

Quitclaim Deed   A deed that operates to release any interest in a property that a person may have, *without a representation that he or she actually has a right in that property*. For example, Sally may use a quitclaim deed to grant Bill her interest in the White House, in Washington, D.C., although she may not actually own, or have any rights to, that particular house.

Real Rate of Return   Your rate of return with a bond consists of two pieces: the interest you've earned on the bond and the actual market value of the bond (it could be above or below face value when you sell it). If the market value of the bond has appreciated, you may have to pay capital gains tax on the rise in value. The interest you earn is taxed like income.

Real Estate   Land and anything permanently attached to it, such as buildings and improvements.

Real Estate Agent   An individual licensed by the state, who acts on behalf of the seller or buyer. For his or her services, the agent receives a commission, which is usually expressed as a percentage of the sales price of a home and is split with his or her real-estate firm. A real estate agent must either be a real estate broker or work for one.

Real Estate Attorney   An attorney who specializes in the purchase and sale of real estate.

Real Estate Broker   An individual who is licensed by the state to act as an agent on behalf of the seller or buyer. For his or her services, the broker receives a commission, which is usually expressed as a percentage of the sales price of a home.

Real Estate Settlement Procedures Act (RESPA)   This federal statute was originally passed in 1974, and contains provisions that govern the way companies involved with a real estate closing must treat each other and the consumer. For example, one section of RESPA requires lenders to give consumers a written good faith estimate within three days of making an application for a loan. Another section of RESPA prohibits title companies from giving referral fees to brokers for steering business to them.

Realtist   A designation given to an agent or broker who is a member of the National Association of Real Estate Brokers.

Realtor   A designation given to a real estate agent or broker who is a member of the National Association of Realtors.

Recording   The process of filing documents at a specific government office. Upon such recording, the document becomes part of the public record.

Redemption Fee   Typically, a charge that's imposed on people who redeem their shares in a mutual fund within a short period. It might be ninety days or three years. Some funds impose a .25 percent redemption fee no matter when you cash out. Why? This is another way for funds to be profitable. But there may be some additional costs if too many people take their money out at exactly the same moment. Funds have to keep some money in cash reserves in case people want to redeem their shares. If too many people want to redeem their shares all at once, the fund would have to sell some stock, perhaps not at the most fortuitous time.

Redlining   Jargon used to describe an illegal practice of discrimination against a particular racial group by real-estate lenders or insurance companies. Redlining occurs when lenders or insurance companies decide certain areas of a community are undesirable for investment, either because the community is poor, has a high level of crime, has too many minorities, or has low property values. Real-estate companies who redline simply refuse to give a mortgage to buyers who want to purchase property in those areas, regardless of their qualifications or creditworthiness. Insurance companies who redline refuse to insure consumers who live in certain neighborhoods.

Regulation M   The revised federal rules that went into effect at the end of 1997. Regulation M standardizes and simplified car leasing forms and language. While it requires dealers to disclose all sorts of information, it does not require them to disclose the money factor (also known as the lease rate).

Regulation Z   Also known as the Truth in Lending Act. Congress determined that lenders must provide a written good-faith estimate of closing costs to all borrowers, and provide them with other written information about the loan.

Replacement Insurance   This guarantees that the insurer will pay for the cost of replacing the home in its current condition up to the policy's limits. This is a less expensive form of homeowner's insurance than *guaranteed replacement cost insurance* (see above), which will pay to put your home in its current condition and meet all current codes as well, and it typically won't pay to bring your home up to current standards.

Reserve   The amount of money set aside by a condo, co-op, or homeowners' association for future capital improvements.

Residual Value   How much the car dealer says the car will be worth at the end of the lease term. Typically, this is not negotiable.

Roth IRA   The Tax Relief Act of 1997 created a Roth IRA, which allows nondeductible, after-tax contributions of up to $2,000 per year. As long as you hold the IRA for at least five years, the distributions are tax-free. In addition, you are not required to make a minimum contribution each year, and there is no age limit for additional contributions. Anyone who earns less than $95,000 (single) or $160,000 (married) may be able to open up a Roth IRA.

Sale-Leaseback   A transaction in which the seller sells property to a buyer, who then leases the property back to the seller. This is accomplished within the same transaction.

Sales Contract   The document by which a buyer contracts to purchase property. Also known as the *purchase contract* or a *contract to purchase*.

Sales Tax   In most areas, a car lease is considered the same as a purchase. So you'll pay sales tax on your purchase. That's one reason to think carefully about where you purchase or lease your vehicle. You might only pay 7.5 percent sales tax instead of 8.75 percent, depending on where you buy or lease your car. And when you're talking about a $20,000 car, saving 1.25 percent means saving $250.

Savings Bond   Backed by the U.S. government, savings bonds (which come in different series, like EE and HH) can be purchased in small amounts, either directly from a bank or from the Treasury Department, or through a broker. They're nontransferable, and are not traded as are other government offerings. In September 1998 the government began selling an inflation-indexed savings bonds. The I-bond guarantees that your return will outpace inflation, and is actually based on the rate of inflation plus a fixed rate of return, perhaps 3 to 3.5 percent.

Savings Incentive Match Plan for Employees (SIMPLE-401(k) or IRA)   A pension plan for employers with 100 or fewer employees (who earn at least $5,000 per year). The employer must match the employee contribution, which is limited to a dollar amount that is indexed for inflation.

Second Mortgage   A mortgage that is obtained after the primary mortgage, and whose rights for repayment are secondary to the first mortgage.

Seller Broker   A broker who has a fiduciary responsibility to the seller. Most brokers are seller brokers, although an increasing number are buyer brokers, who have a fiduciary responsibility to the buyer.

Settlement Statement   A statement that details the monies paid out and received by the buyer and seller at closing.

Shared Appreciation Mortgage   A relatively new mortgage used to help first-time buyers who might not qualify for conventional financing. In a shared appreciation mortgage, the lender offers a below-market interest rate in return for a portion of the profits made by the homeowner when the property is sold. Before entering into a shared appreciation mortgage, be sure to have your real-estate attorney review the documentation.

Simplified Employee Pension (SEP-IRA)   This is a type of pension plan used by small businesses. The employer's contributions are excluded from the employee's taxable salary and may not exceed 15 percent of the employee's salary or the current dollar amount set by the government, whichever is less.

Social Security   Under the Social Security Act of 1935, the government established the Social Security Administration to provide retirement benefits, disability income, and Medicare for working individuals and their spouses.

Special Assessment   An additional charge levied by a condo or co-op board in order to pay for capital improvements or other unforeseen expenses.

Specialty Funds   A mutual fund that specializes in one particular market sector or industry, or even in a specific piece of an industry.

Spin-Off   A portion of a company that has divided itself into several pieces, giving new shares in the company to current shareholders. Your 100 shares of stock in one company may turn into 300 shares if the company divides itself three ways, and rewards stockholders with one share in each new company for each share currently held.

Standard Deduction   If you decide not to itemize your deductions, or if you can't, you may opt for the standard deduction, an amount set by the government and indexed for inflation.

Stock Rights   Your right as a shareholder to purchase new shares, often at a discount. Sometimes you'll see this if you have an account at a savings-and-loan that announces it intends to go public. Account holders are offered the right to purchase shares of stock in the company before the initial public offering.

Subagent   A broker who brings the buyer to the property. Although subagents would appear to be working for the buyer (a subagent usually ferries the buyer around, showing him or her properties), they are paid by the seller and have a fiduciary responsibility to the seller. Subagency is often confusing to first-time buyers, who think that because the subagent shows them property, the subagent is "their" agent, rather than the seller's.

Subdivision   The division of a large piece of property into several smaller pieces. Usually a developer or a group of developers will build single-family or duplex homes of a similar design and cost within one subdivision.

Subvented Lease   A car lease that's subsidized (typically by the auto manufacturer) in order to get rid of a certain kind of car. Subvented leases can be exceptional deals, and they are often the only way that leasing may be cheaper than owning (unless you pay cash, in which case a well-negotiated car purchase will almost certainly be cheaper than any lease you could get).

Surrender Value   See *cash surrender value*, above.

Tax Audit   A formal examination of your tax return by IRS auditors.

Tax Bracket   A range of income that must pay a certain level of taxes. The higher your income, the higher your tax bracket, and the more tax you pay.

Tax Credit   A dollar-for-dollar amount subtracted directly from the taxes you owe.

Tax Deduction   See **Deduction,** above.

Tax Lien   A lien that is attached to property if the owner does not pay his or her real-estate taxes or federal income taxes. If overdue property taxes are not paid, the owner's property might be sold at auction for the amount owed in back taxes.

Tax Shelter   An investment entered into for the primary purpose of lowering your tax burden.

Taxable Income   Your gross earnings minus deductions and exclusions.

Tenancy by the Entirety   A type of ownership whereby both the husband and wife together own the complete property. Each spouse has an ownership interest in the property they live in as their marital residence and, as a result, creditors of one spouse cannot force the sale of the home to pay back his or her debts without the other spouse's consent. There are rights of survivorship whereby upon the death of one spouse, the other spouse would immediately inherit the entire property.

Tenants in Common   A type of ownership in which two or more parties have an undivided interest in the property. The owners may or may not have equal shares of ownership, and there are no rights of survivorship. However, each owner retains the right to sell his or her share in the property as he or she sees fit.

Tender Offer   When a company wants to take over another company, it will offer a price per share that is typically above the market price. You will be asked to tender, or surrender, your shares for the higher price. In reality, after the tender offer is made, the market price for your stock will usually go up and match the offer. (If it doesn't match the offer, there is some concern in the market that the deal may not go through.)

Term (Bonds)   Short-term bonds run up to three years in length. Intermediate bonds are from three to ten years in length. Long-term bonds run up to thirty years in length. Generally, the bonds that pay the highest interest rate are long-term bonds. However, you'll only earn an extra percentage point or so on your money and have to tie it up for a long period. Financial planners say a better bet is to purchase intermediate-term bonds, which are more flexible.

Term (Car Lease)   How long the car lease lasts. Generally, you won't want to get a car lease for longer than three years. Too many things can start to go wrong with a leased car in its fourth or fifth year, and the likelihood that you'll get some nicks and dings—for which you're liable—increases.

Title   Refers to the ownership of a particular piece of property.

Title Company   The corporation or company that insures the status of title on real estate (called title insurance) at a closing, and may handle other aspects of the real estate closing.

Title Insurance   Insurance that protects the lender and the property owner against losses arising from undisclosed defects or problems with the title to property.

Total Return   Your total return is your dividends plus the gain or loss in the price of the company's stock. If the stock rises 5 percent and your dividends are 2 percent, your total return is 7 percent.

Transaction Fees   The costs mutual funds incur when they buy and sell shares of stock on the open market.

Treasuries   The federal government offers three types of products to raise money: Treasury bills (also known as a T-bills), Treasury notes, and Treasury bonds. Uncle Sam uses the money raised from the sale of these three products to pay for social and spending programs. Collectively, this debt is our national debt. It is considered fail-proof, since it is backed by the U.S. Government.

Treasury Bills (T-Bills)   These are government-backed securities, with a minimum purchase price of $1,000. They are offered in three-month, six-month, and twelve-month lengths. You buy the T-bill at a discount, which, when divided by the effective cost, equals your rate of interest. (So if you purchase a $10,000 T-bill for $9,300, your interest rate is $700 ÷ $9,300 = .08, or 8 percent.) The discount is deposited immediately into your account, and the rest of the face value arrives on the day the bond matures. You have the option of rolling over your T-bill for another period. Since T-bills, like all offerings from the Treasury Department, are backed by the full faith and credit of the U.S. Government, they're considered just about the safest investments around.

Trust Account   An account used by brokers and escrow agents, in which funds for another individual are held separately, not commingled with other funds.

12(b)-1 Fees   These are a mutual fund's marketing expenses. They include everything from the price of printing brochures to the cost of entertaining or compensating brokers who put their clients into the fund.

Umbrella Liability Policy   This insures losses in excess of amounts covered by other liability insurance policies; it also protects the insured in many situations not covered by the usual liability polices.

Underwriter   One who underwrites a loan for another. Your lender will have an investor underwrite your loan.

Universal Life Insurance   A flexible premium life insurance policy under which the policyholder may change the death benefit from time to time (with satisfactory evidence of insurability for increases), vary the amount or timing of premium payments, and choose the investment vehicle for his or her premiums. Premiums (less expense charges and commissions) are credited to a policy account from which mortality charges are deducted and to which interest is credited at a rate that may change from time to time.

Variable Interest Rate   An interest rate that rises and falls according to a particular economic indicator, such as Treasury bills.

Viatical Settlement   Payment of a portion of the proceeds from life insurance to an insured who is terminally ill.

Void   Describes a contract or document that is not enforceable.

Voluntary Lien   A lien, such as a mortgage, that a homeowner elects to grant to a lender.

Waiver   The surrender or relinquishment of a particular right, claim, or privilege.

Warrant   Sometimes, when you buy preferred stock or bonds of speculative companies, you get a warrant, or the right to buy additional shares of stock at a predetermined price. This sounds great, but the company usually has the right to call in the warrants, forcing you to exercise them (i.e., buy stock at the current price) or receive a few cents for each warrant you hold.

Warranty, Home   A legally binding promise given to the buyer at closing by the seller, generally regarding the condition of the home, property, or other related matter.

Wash Sale   If you sell stocks and repurchase them within thirty days prior to or after the sale, you may lose certain tax advantages, according to IRS rules.

Withholding   An ongoing deduction from your paycheck that is sent by your employer on your behalf to the IRS.

Withholding Allowance   One withholding allowance is available for each personal and dependent exemption that you're entitled to take. You may also take additional exemptions to compensate for deductions and credits you plan to use. You may change your withholding allowances during the year if your income will be higher or lower than you planned.

Wrap Accounts   Your broker might offer to wrap your mutual funds in with other investments you own, and keep an eye out on all of it, for a 1-to-3-percent wrap account fee. Another wrap account is a mutual fund that has no up-front load, but charges a fixed percentage of assets each year to cover the cost of the commission, management, and expenses.

Yield to Call   If interest rates go down, your bond issuer will want to refinance his debt. That means he'll call in your bond as soon as he can. If your bond has five years until the call date, you'll want to calculate the yield to call, since the bond issuer may not let the bond mature.

Yield to Maturity   If you hold a bond until it matures, and reinvest every interest payment at the interest rate on your bond, you will end up with your yield to maturity. If you spend your interest payments, or reinvest them at a lower rate (as in a passbook savings account), your yield to maturity will be less. If you invest them at a higher rate, your yield to maturity will be higher.

Zero Coupon Bonds   These pay zero interest throughout the bond term. You buy the bond, however, at a steep discount that includes the implied interest rate. For example, a $1,000 bond paying 8 percent might be purchased for $456. At the date of maturity, you'd collect $544 in interest. The Treasury Department offers zeros (as they're commonly called), as do municipalities and some corporations.

Zoning   The right of a local municipal government to decide how different areas of the municipality will be used. Zoning ordinances are the laws that govern the use of the land.

Acknowledgments

With a book such as this, the author gets to take sole credit. In truth, it is the work of many talented individuals, including hundreds of financial experts and consumers I've interviewed throughout the years, who willingly shared their information and tips and took the time to talk with me about their experiences. April Powell provided excellent research assistance, finding and organizing more than a thousand pages of materials.

I'm grateful for the unwavering friendship of my agent, Alice and Martell, and my attorney Ralph Martire. I am also grateful for the work of the excellent editorial staff at Three Rivers Press and Crown Publishers, including Betsy Rapoport, Steve Ross, Brian Belfiglio, and others who work so hard to make sure these books look beautiful and read well.

My family continues to offer their support for all that I do, for which I can never thank them enough. And, finally, I would have never finished this book without the unstinting help of my husband and best friend, Samuel J. Tamkin, the world's best real-estate attorney, who continues to believe all my wildest dreams will come true.

Index